Never Quit!

"...I am thy God: I will strengthen thee."—
Isaiah 41:10.

1,000 SOURCES OF STRENGTH FROM GOD'S WORD

BY LINDSAY AND MARILYN TERRY

SWORD of the LORD
PUBLISHERS

Post Office Box 1099 • Murfreesboro, Tennessee 37133

Printed and Bound in the United States of America

CONTENTS

PREFACE

Never give in, never give in, never, never, never, never—in nothing, great or small, large or petty—never give in except to convictions of honour and good sense.

The above was Winston Churchill's admonition to the boys of England's Harrow School, on October 29, 1941. He had attended the school during his early years. England was in the throes of World War II, and so he also urged the students to pray for extra courage and expressed to them his gratitude to God.

I, of course, don't know if Churchill ever really trusted Christ as his personal Saviour, but history tells that in his childhood years his governess, Elizabeth Everest, whom he affectionately called Woom, taught him to pray. She also taught him the Scriptures and helped him memorize many favorite verses as well as meaningful, long passages. He won awards for reciting large portions of the Bible. It must have been from God's Word that he learned convictions and how to stand and fight if the cause be noble—to never, never, never, NEVER QUIT! When he was approximately sixteen years of age, Churchill became very upset with his parents for dismissing his beloved Woom. They thought Winston no longer needed a governess.

In later years, as Great Britain's Prime Minister, and with the United States on his side, he led his beloved country, though battered and torn from the ravages of bombing, in the defeat of Hitler.

Christians, we are in a warfare with the Devil, and there must be victory; there can be victory if we NEVER QUIT! I have been through periods of spiritual warfare in my life when I saw a pressing need to turn to our Heavenly Father. During those times the Bible became very precious, and today it remains a "Safe Harbor" and a source of strength.

PREFACE

On a number of occasions during the last eight to ten years, I have gone through the New Testament as well as many parts of the Old Testament several times. It has been a wonderful journey each time. I have realized, at times, that I had memorized portions of Scripture without even knowing it. The Word of God helps us to learn to *never quit!* It is comforting to know that God says, *"Fear thou not; for I am with thee: be not dismayed; for I am thy God: I will strengthen thee; yea, I will help thee; yea, I will uphold thee with the right hand of my righteousness."*

In this book Marilyn and I have tried to include topics that will be helpful to most Christians during special times in their lives. Since both of us have counseled countless adults and taught the Bible in Sunday school, Bible study groups, church services, on radio and television programs, and to our children over a period of more than forty years, we believe that we have developed a feel for what subjects are most needful. The list is not exhaustive, but space allows only certain topics.

As a child of God, you should tuck selections of these gems away into your heart by committing them to memory. If you have never trusted Christ as your personal Saviour, then you can find out how to know Him by reading the Scriptures found in the chapter titled "Salvation" or by reading God's plan of salvation on the page following this preface. The Bible not only lights your world but, as the Sword of the Spirit, it also provides you with weapons against Satan.

As you read the Scriptures addressing varying subjects, you will get the concept and the assurance that each passage or verse is supported and enhanced by the preceding and the following ones.

May this book be a constant help to you as you refer to it from time to time. It should not take the place of your regular Bible study, but can be of special help in particular times of need. It can also prepare you to help others with the subjects mentioned on these pages.

GOD'S PLAN FOR MY SALVATION

In order to know Christ as my Saviour, I must acknowledge the truth of the following:

1. I must realize that in my present condition I am a sinner before God.

"For all have sinned, and come short of the glory of God."—Romans 3:23.

"As it is written, There is none righteous, no, not one."—Romans 3:10.

2. I cannot save myself from eternal punishment in Hell.

"For the wages of sin is death; but the gift of God is eternal life through Jesus Christ our Lord."—Romans 6:23.

"And as it is appointed unto men once to die, but after this the judgment."—Hebrews 9:27.

3. Christ has paid for my sins and taken my punishment with His death on the cross.

"But God commendeth his love toward us, in that, while we were yet sinners, Christ died for us."—Romans 5:8.

"For God so loved the world, that he gave his only begotten Son, that whosoever believeth in him should not perish, but have everlasting life."—John 3:16.

4. I must accept His crucifixion as payment for my sins, personally.

"For whosoever shall call upon the name of the Lord shall be saved."—Romans 10:13.

"But as many as received him, to them gave he power to

become the sons of God, even to them that believe on his name.''—John 1:12.

If you believe the above Scriptures, would you bow your head right where you are, right now, and ask Christ to come into your heart and save you? Turn your whole life over to Him as Lord.

You might pray something like this:

Dear Lord Jesus, I confess that I am a guilty sinner and that I need to be saved. I believe that You died on the cross to pay my sin debt. Please forgive my sins, come into my heart and save my soul. I turn my life over to You right now. Help me to live for You the rest of my life. Amen.

If you have received Christ as your personal Saviour, welcome to the family of God! Please find a good church where the Bible is taught and tell the pastor what you have done. Begin to tell others about your newfound faith in Christ.

ABORTION

"For thou hast possessed my reins: thou hast covered me in my mother's womb. I will praise thee; for I am fearfully and wonderfully made: marvellous are thy works; and that my soul knoweth right well."—Psalm 139:13,14.

"As thou knowest not what is the way of the spirit, nor how the bones do grow in the womb of her that is with child: even so thou knowest not the works of God who maketh all."—Ecclesiastes 11:5.

"Listen, O isles, unto me; and hearken, ye people, from far; The LORD hath called me from the womb; from the bowels of my mother hath he made mention of my name."—Isaiah 49:1.

"Thus saith the LORD that made thee, and formed thee from the womb, which will help thee; Fear not, O Jacob, my servant; and thou, Jesurun, whom I have chosen."—Isaiah 44:2.

The life that has begun in the womb
of the mother is brought to a
swift and deadly end.

"And Isaac intreated the LORD for his wife, because she was barren: and the LORD was intreated of him, and Rebekah his wife conceived. And the children struggled together within her; and she said, If it be so, why am I thus? And she went to enquire of the LORD. And the LORD said unto her, Two nations are in thy womb, and two manner of people shall be separated from thy bowels; and the one people shall be stronger than the other people; and the elder shall serve the younger."—Genesis 25:21–23.

1

"If men strive, and hurt a woman with child, so that her fruit depart from her, and yet no mischief follow: he shall be surely punished, according as the woman's husband will lay upon him; and he shall pay as the judges determine. And if any mischief follow, then thou shalt give life for life, Eye for eye, tooth for tooth, hand for hand, foot for foot, Burning for burning, wound for wound, stripe for stripe."— Exodus 21:22–25.

*"Before I formed thee in the belly I knew thee; and before thou camest forth out of the womb I sanctified thee, and I ordained thee a prophet unto the nations."—*Jeremiah 1:5.

*"And now, saith the LORD that formed me from the womb to be his servant, to bring Jacob again to him, Though Israel be not gathered, yet shall I be glorious in the eyes of the LORD, and my God shall be my strength."—*Isaiah 49:5.

*"But when it pleased God, who separated me from my mother's womb, and called me by his grace."—*Galatians 1:15.

*"Can a woman forget her sucking child, that she should not have compassion on the son of her womb? yea, they may forget, yet will I not forget thee."—*Isaiah 49:15.

*"And it came to pass, that, when Elisabeth heard the salutation of Mary, the babe leaped in her womb; and Elisabeth was filled with the Holy Ghost....For, lo, as soon as the voice of thy salutation sounded in mine ears, the babe leaped in my womb for joy."—*Luke 1:41, 44.

The moment the Holy Ghost came to Mary and she conceived, the Child was there. The Lord Jesus Christ was present within her as much then as He ever was.

–Sidney W. Hunter

ANGELS

"For he shall give his angels charge over thee, to keep thee in all thy ways. They shall bear thee up in their hands, lest thou dash thy foot against a stone."—Psalm 91:11,12.

God's wonderful created beings that have the
privilege of serving Him continually,
often on our behalf.

"Be not forgetful to entertain strangers: for thereby some have entertained angels unawares."—Hebrews 13:2.

"And it came to pass, that the beggar died, and was carried by the angels into Abraham's bosom: the rich man also died, and was buried."—Luke 16:22.

"Though I speak with the tongues of men and of angels, and have not charity, I am become as sounding brass, or a tinkling cymbal."—I Corinthians 13:1.

"And all that sat in the council, looking stedfastly on him, saw his face as it had been the face of an angel."—Acts 6:15.

"Praise ye him, all his angels: praise ye him, all his hosts."—Psalm 148:2.

"For thou hast made him a little lower than the angels, and hast crowned him with glory and honour."—Psalm 8:5.

"And, behold, the angel of the Lord came upon him, and a light shined in the prison: and he smote Peter on the side, and raised him up, saying, Arise up quickly. And his chains fell off from his hands."—Acts 12:7.

3

"For there stood by me this night the angel of God, whose I am, and whom I serve, Saying, Fear not, Paul; thou must be brought before Cæsar: and, lo, God hath given thee all them that sail with thee."—Acts 27:23,24.

"But ye are come unto mount Sion, and unto the city of the living God, the heavenly Jerusalem, and to an innumerable company of angels."—Hebrews 12:22.

"The chariots of God are twenty thousand, even thousands of angels: the Lord is among them, as in Sinai, in the holy place."—Psalm 68:17.

"For the Son of man shall come in the glory of his Father with his angels; and then he shall reward every man according to his works."—Matthew 16:27.

"The same shall drink of the wine of the wrath of God, which is poured out without mixture into the cup of his indignation; and he shall be tormented with fire and brimstone in the presence of the holy angels, and in the presence of the Lamb."—Revelation 14:10.

"And when they were departed, behold, the angel of the Lord appeareth to Joseph in a dream, saying, Arise, and take the young child and his mother, and flee into Egypt, and be thou there until I bring thee word: for Herod will seek the young child to destroy him."—Matthew 2:13.

The angels may have wider spheres of action and nobler forms of duty than ourselves, but truth and right to them and to us are one and the same thing.

—E. H. Chapin

ANGER

"Wherefore, my beloved brethren, let every man be swift to hear, slow to speak, slow to wrath: For the wrath of man worketh not the righteousness of God."—James 1:19,20.

"A soft answer turneth away wrath: but grievous words stir up anger."—Proverbs 15:1.

"Be ye angry, and sin not: let not the sun go down upon your wrath."—Ephesians 4:26.

"A man of great wrath shall suffer punishment: for if thou deliver him, yet thou must do it again."—Proverbs 19:19.

"He that is soon angry dealeth foolishly: and a man of wicked devices is hated."—Proverbs 14:17.

There are some things we should become angry with, while keeping it under control. However, we often let anger get the better of us, which is dangerous.

"For a bishop must be blameless, as the steward of God; not selfwilled, not soon angry, not given to wine, no striker, not given to filthy lucre."—Titus 1:7.

"The heart knoweth his own bitterness; and a stranger doth not intermeddle with his joy."—Proverbs 14:10.

"Fathers, provoke not your children to anger, lest they be discouraged."—Colossians 3:21.

"An angry man stirreth up strife, and a furious man aboundeth in transgression."—Proverbs 29:22.

5

Never Quit!

"Cease from anger, and forsake wrath: fret not thyself in any wise to do evil." — Psalm 37:8.

"The discretion of a man deferreth his anger; and it is his glory to pass over a transgression." — Proverbs 19:11.

"Wrath is cruel, and anger is outrageous; but who is able to stand before envy?" — Proverbs 27:4.

"Be not hasty in thy spirit to be angry: for anger resteth in the bosom of fools." — Ecclesiastes 7:9.

"Let all bitterness, and wrath, and anger, and clamour, and evil speaking, be put away from you, with all malice." — Ephesians 4:31.

"But now ye also put off all these; anger, wrath, malice, blasphemy, filthy communication out of your mouth." — Colossians 3:8.

Anger is an acid that can do more harm to the vessel in which it is stored than to anything on which it is poured.

–Mark Twain

ATTITUDE

"And whatsoever ye do in word or deed, do all in the name of the Lord Jesus, giving thanks to God and the Father by him."—Colossians 3:17.

"Beloved, think it not strange concerning the fiery trial which is to try you, as though some strange thing happened unto you: But rejoice, inasmuch as ye are partakers of Christ's sufferings; that, when his glory shall be revealed, ye may be glad also with exceeding joy."—I Peter 4:12,13.

"Finally, brethren, whatsoever things are true, whatsoever things are honest, whatsoever things are just, whatsoever things are pure, whatsoever things are lovely, whatsoever things are of good report; if there be any virtue, and if there be any praise, think on these things. Those things, which ye have both learned, and received, and heard, and seen in me, do: and the God of peace shall be with you."—Philippians 4:8,9.

"Let this mind be in you, which was also in Christ Jesus: Who, being in the form of God, thought it not robbery to be equal with God: But made himself of no reputation, and took upon him the form of a servant, and was made in the likeness of men: And being found in fashion as a man, he humbled himself, and became obedient unto death, even the death of the cross."—Philippians 2:5–8.

Each morning when we rise, our all-important attitudes toward that day begin to form. Our attitudes in responding to events that happen during the day are often much more important than the events.

"Be of good courage, and he shall strengthen your heart, all ye that hope in the LORD."—Psalm 31:24.

7

"Forasmuch then as Christ hath suffered for us in the flesh, arm yourselves likewise with the same mind: for he that hath suffered in the flesh hath ceased from sin; That he no longer should live the rest of his time in the flesh to the lusts of men, but to the will of God."—I Peter 4:1, 2.

"For we preach not ourselves, but Christ Jesus the Lord; and ourselves your servants for Jesus' sake. For God, who commanded the light to shine out of darkness, hath shined in our hearts, to give the light of the knowledge of the glory of God in the face of Jesus Christ."—II Corinthians 4:5, 6.

"Yea, though I walk through the valley of the shadow of death, I will fear no evil: for thou art with me; thy rod and thy staff they comfort me. Thou preparest a table before me in the presence of mine enemies: thou anointest my head with oil; my cup runneth over. Surely goodness and mercy shall follow me all the days of my life: and I will dwell in the house of the LORD for ever."—Psalm 23:4–6.

"Many are the afflictions of the righteous: but the LORD delivereth him out of them all."—Psalm 34:19.

What life each day means to you is not determined by what life brings to you, but rather what attitude you bring to life.

–Beverly Hyles

AUTHORITY OF CHRIST

"Jesus answered, Thou couldest have no power at all against me, except it were given thee from above: therefore he that delivered me unto thee hath the greater sin."— John 19:11.

"Then cometh the end, when he shall have delivered up the kingdom to God, even the Father; when he shall have put down all rule and all authority and power."— I Corinthians 15:24.

Each of us must quickly realize that there is an Authority
to whom we should submit in order for our lives
to be happy and successful.

"Ye call me Master and Lord: and ye say well; for so I am."—John 13:13.

"Who is the image of the invisible God, the firstborn of every creature: For by him were all things created, that are in heaven, and that are in earth, visible and invisible, whether they be thrones, or dominions, or principalities, or powers: all things were created by him, and for him: And he is before all things, and by him all things consist. And he is the head of the body, the church: who is the beginning, the firstborn from the dead; that in all things he might have the preeminence. For it pleased the Father that in him should all fulness dwell; And, having made peace through the blood of his cross, by him to reconcile all things unto himself; by him, I say, whether they be things in earth, or things in heaven."—Colossians 1:15–20.

"For in him dwelleth all the fulness of the Godhead bodily. And ye are complete in him, which is the head of all principality and power."—Colossians 2:9,10.

9

"Submit yourselves to every ordinance of man for the Lord's sake: whether it be to the king, as supreme; Or unto governors, as unto them that are sent by him for the punishment of evildoers, and for the praise of them that do well. For so is the will of God, that with well doing ye may put to silence the ignorance of foolish men: As free, and not using your liberty for a cloke of maliciousness, but as the servants of God. Honour all men. Love the brotherhood. Fear God. Honour the king."—I Peter 2:13–17.

"Looking for that blessed hope, and the glorious appearing of the great God and our Saviour Jesus Christ; Who gave himself for us, that he might redeem us from all iniquity, and purify unto himself a peculiar people, zealous of good works. These things speak, and exhort, and rebuke with all authority. Let no man despise thee."—Titus 2:13–15.

"Wives, submit yourselves unto your own husbands, as unto the Lord. For the husband is the head of the wife, even as Christ is the head of the church: and he is the saviour of the body."—Ephesians 5:22,23.

"And Jesus came and spake unto them, saying, All power is given unto me in heaven and in earth. Go ye therefore, and teach all nations, baptizing them in the name of the Father, and of the Son, and of the Holy Ghost: Teaching them to observe all things whatsoever I have commanded you: and, lo, I am with you alway, even unto the end of the world. Amen."—Matthew 28:18–20.

As Christians we represent Jesus Christ; therefore, we must speak His words and express His sentiments concerning the issues that face us, if we are going to represent Him rightly.

–Shelton Smith

BITTERNESS

"Let all bitterness, and wrath, and anger, and clamour, and evil speaking, be put away from you, with all malice: And be ye kind one to another, tenderhearted, forgiving one another, even as God for Christ's sake hath forgiven you."—Ephesians 4:31, 32.

"Follow peace with all men, and holiness, without which no man shall see the Lord: Looking diligently lest any man fail of the grace of God; lest any root of bitterness springing up trouble you, and thereby many be defiled."—Hebrews 12:14, 15.

"Bless them which persecute you: bless, and curse not."—Romans 12:14.

"For even hereunto were ye called: because Christ also suffered for us, leaving us an example, that ye should follow his steps: Who did no sin, neither was guile found in his mouth: Who, when he was reviled, reviled not again; when he suffered, he threatened not; but committed himself to him that judgeth righteously."—I Peter 2:21–23.

Little do many of us realize the toll that bitterness
takes on our bodies, minds and souls.
It is a poison like no other.

"But if ye have bitter envying and strife in your hearts, glory not, and lie not against the truth. This wisdom descendeth not from above, but is earthly, sensual, devilish."—James 3:14, 15.

"Out of the same mouth proceedeth blessing and cursing. My brethren, these things ought not so to be."—James 3:10.

11

"Recompense to no man evil for evil. Provide things honest in the sight of all men."—Romans 12:17.

"Woe unto him that striveth with his Maker! Let the potsherd strive with the potsherds of the earth. Shall the clay say to him that fashioneth it, What makest thou? or thy work, He hath no hands?"—Isaiah 45:9.

"A foolish son is a grief to his father, and bitterness to her that bare him."—Proverbs 17:25.

"Husbands, love your wives, and be not bitter against them."—Colossians 3:19.

"Whose mouth is full of cursing and bitterness: Their feet are swift to shed blood: Destruction and misery are in their ways: And the way of peace have they not known: There is no fear of God before their eyes."—Romans 3:14–18.

"Repent therefore of this thy wickedness, and pray God, if perhaps the thought of thine heart may be forgiven thee. For I perceive that thou art in the gall of bitterness, and in the bond of iniquity."—Acts 8:22,23.

"Hear my voice, O God, in my prayer: preserve my life from fear of the enemy. Hide me from the secret counsel of the wicked; from the insurrection of the workers of iniquity: Who whet their tongue like a sword, and bend their bows to shoot their arrows, even bitter words."—Psalm 64:1–3.

**Few things are more bitter than to feel bitter.
A man's venom poisons himself
more than his victim.**

–Charles Buxton

CHARITY

"I am distressed for thee, my brother Jonathan: very pleasant hast thou been unto me: thy love to me was wonderful, passing the love of women."—II Samuel 1:26.

"Let no man seek his own, but every man another's wealth."—I Corinthians 10:24.

"Put on therefore, as the elect of God, holy and beloved, bowels of mercies, kindness, humbleness of mind, meekness, longsuffering; Forbearing one another, and forgiving one another, if any man have a quarrel against any: even as Christ forgave you, so also do ye. And above all these things put on charity, which is the bond of perfectness."— Colossians 3:12–14.

A great source of happiness for those who have a genuine, godly love for his or her friends.

"And above all things have fervent charity among yourselves: for charity shall cover the multitude of sins."— I Peter 4:8.

"But whoso keepeth his word, in him verily is the love of God perfected: hereby know we that we are in him."— I John 2:5.

"For this is the message that ye heard from the beginning, that we should love one another."—I John 3:11.

"We know that we have passed from death unto life, because we love the brethren. He that loveth not his brother abideth in death."—I John 3:14.

"Beloved, let us love one another: for love is of God; and every one that loveth is born of God, and knoweth God. He that loveth not knoweth not God; for God is love."— I John 4:7, 8.

"This is my commandment, That ye love one another, as I have loved you. Greater love hath no man than this, that a man lay down his life for his friends."—John 15:12, 13.

"No man hath seen God at any time. If we love one another, God dwelleth in us, and his love is perfected in us."—I John 4:12.

"And thou shalt love the Lord thy God with all thy heart, and with all thy soul, and with all thy mind, and with all thy strength: this is the first commandment. And the second is like, namely this, Thou shalt love thy neighbour as thyself. There is none other commandment greater than these. And the scribe said unto him, Well, Master, thou hast said the truth: for there is one God; and there is none other but he: And to love him with all the heart, and with all the understanding, and with all the soul, and with all the strength, and to love his neighbour as himself, is more than all whole burnt-offerings and sacrifices."—Mark 12:30–33.

"And we have known and believed the love that God hath to us. God is love; and he that dwelleth in love dwelleth in God, and God in him."—I John 4:16.

"And this commandment have we from him, That he who loveth God love his brother also."—I John 4:21.

Help me in all the work I do
To ever be sincere and true,
And know that all I'd do for you
Must needs be done for others.

—C. D. Meigs

14

CHILDREN

"Children, obey your parents in all things: for this is well pleasing unto the Lord."—Colossians 3:20.

"Obey them that have the rule over you, and submit yourselves: for they watch for your souls, as they that must give account, that they may do it with joy, and not with grief: for that is unprofitable for you."—Hebrews 13:17.

"Correct thy son, and he shall give thee rest; yea, he shall give delight unto thy soul."—Proverbs 29:17.

Children are our greatest treasure, yet many
children are in dire need—a great mission
field in our world, abroad and at home.

"Children, obey your parents in the Lord: for this is right. Honour thy father and mother; which is the first commandment with promise; That it may be well with thee, and thou mayest live long on the earth."—Ephesians 6:1–3.

"Honour thy father and thy mother: that thy days may be long upon the land which the LORD thy God giveth thee."—Exodus 20:12.

"When my father and my mother forsake me, then the LORD will take me up."—Psalm 27:10.

"Whoso robbeth his father or his mother, and saith, It is no transgression; the same is the companion of a destroyer."—Proverbs 28:24.

"Foolishness is bound in the heart of a child; but the rod of correction shall drive it far from him."—Proverbs 22:15.

15

"The father of the righteous shall greatly rejoice: and he that begetteth a wise child shall have joy of him. Thy father and thy mother shall be glad, and she that bare thee shall rejoice."—Proverbs 23:24,25.

"For I know him, that he will command his children and his household after him, and they shall keep the way of the Lord, to do justice and judgment; that the Lord may bring upon Abraham that which he hath spoken of him."—Genesis 18:19.

"Ye shall fear every man his mother, and his father, and keep my sabbaths: I am the Lord your God."—Leviticus 19:3.

"Only take heed to thyself, and keep thy soul diligently, lest thou forget the things which thine eyes have seen, and lest they depart from thy heart all the days of thy life: but teach them thy sons, and thy sons' sons."—Deuteronomy 4:9.

"Behold, the third time I am ready to come to you; and I will not be burdensome to you: for I seek not your's, but you: for the children ought not to lay up for the parents, but the parents for the children."—II Corinthians 12:14.

"Whoso curseth his father or his mother, his lamp shall be put out in obscure darkness."—Proverbs 20:20.

**Kids really brighten a household.
They never turn the lights off.**

–Ralph Bus

CHOICES

"And if it seem evil unto you to serve the LORD, choose you this day whom ye will serve; whether the gods which your fathers served that were on the other side of the flood, or the gods of the Amorites, in whose land ye dwell: but as for me and my house, we will serve the LORD."—Joshua 24:15.

"And thine ears shall hear a word behind thee, saying, This is the way, walk ye in it, when ye turn to the right hand, and when ye turn to the left."—Isaiah 30:21.

"Blessed is the man that walketh not in the counsel of the ungodly, nor standeth in the way of sinners, nor sitteth in the seat of the scornful."—Psalm 1:1.

"For this God is our God for ever and ever: he will be our guide even unto death."—Psalm 48:14.

"Trust in the LORD with all thine heart; and lean not unto thine own understanding. In all thy ways acknowledge him, and he shall direct thy paths."—Proverbs 3:5,6.

The right choices sometimes are most difficult, but they
bring rewards that make them all worthwhile.

"Nevertheless I am continually with thee: thou hast holden me by my right hand. Thou shalt guide me with thy counsel, and afterward receive me to glory."—Psalm 73:23,24.

"A man's heart deviseth his way: but the LORD directeth his steps."—Proverbs 16:9.

"I will instruct thee and teach thee in the way which thou shalt go: I will guide thee with mine eye."—Psalm 32:8.

17

"I the LORD have called thee in righteousness, and will hold thine hand, and will keep thee, and give thee for a covenant of the people, for a light of the Gentiles."—Isaiah 42:6.

"Be strong and of a good courage, fear not, nor be afraid of them: for the LORD thy God, he it is that doth go with thee; he will not fail thee, nor forsake thee."—Deuteronomy 31:6.

"Thy word is a lamp unto my feet, and a light unto my path. I have sworn, and I will perform it, that I will keep thy righteous judgments."—Psalm 119:105,106.

"And this I pray, that your love may abound yet more and more in knowledge and in all judgment; That ye may approve things that are excellent; that ye may be sincere and without offence till the day of Christ."—Philippians 1:9,10.

"I have taught thee in the way of wisdom; I have led thee in right paths. When thou goest, thy steps shall not be straitened; and when thou runnest, thou shalt not stumble."—Proverbs 4:11,12.

It is a poor and disgraceful thing not to be able to reply, with some degree of certainty, to the simple questions, "What will you be? What will you do?"

—John Foster

CHRISTIAN MATURITY

"How much better is it to get wisdom than gold! and to get understanding rather to be chosen than silver!"—Proverbs 16:16.

"We are bound to thank God always for you, brethren, as it is meet, because that your faith groweth exceedingly, and the charity of every one of you all toward each other aboundeth."—II Thessalonians 1:3.

"Finally, my brethren, be strong in the Lord, and in the power of his might. Put on the whole armour of God, that ye may be able to stand against the wiles of the devil. For we wrestle not against flesh and blood, but against principalities, against powers, against the rulers of the darkness of this world, against spiritual wickedness in high places. Wherefore take unto you the whole armour of God, that ye may be able to withstand in the evil day, and having done all, to stand. Stand therefore, having your loins girt about with truth, and having on the breastplate of righteousness."—Ephesians 6:10–14.

"Call unto me, and I will answer thee, and shew thee great and mighty things, which thou knowest not."—Jeremiah 33:3.

With the Bible as our guide, we strive to become more Christlike in our daily lives.

"But grow in grace, and in the knowledge of our Lord and Saviour Jesus Christ. To him be glory both now and for ever. Amen."—II Peter 3:18.

"A man's heart deviseth his way: but the LORD directeth his steps."—Proverbs 16:9.

"But continue thou in the things which thou hast learned and hast been assured of, knowing of whom thou hast learned them; And that from a child thou hast known the holy scriptures, which are able to make thee wise unto salvation through faith which is in Christ Jesus."—II Timothy 3:14, 15.

"The heart of the wise teacheth his mouth, and addeth learning to his lips."—Proverbs 16:23.

"Study to shew thyself approved unto God, a workman that needeth not to be ashamed, rightly dividing the word of truth."—II Timothy 2:15.

"That Christ may dwell in your hearts by faith; that ye, being rooted and grounded in love, May be able to comprehend with all saints what is the breadth, and length, and depth, and height; And to know the love of Christ, which passeth knowledge, that ye might be filled with all the fulness of God."—Ephesians 3:17–19.

"As newborn babes, desire the sincere milk of the word, that ye may grow thereby: If so be ye have tasted that the Lord is gracious."—I Peter 2:2, 3.

"Commit thy works unto the LORD, and thy thoughts shall be established."—Proverbs 16:3.

"Apply thine heart unto instruction, and thine ears to the words of knowledge."—Proverbs 23:12.

We may have a goal of reaching maturity as a Christian, but no matter how diligent our journey, we just never seem to arrive.

–Lindsay Terry

CHRISTIAN MUSIC

"Praise him with the sound of the trumpet: praise him with the psaltery and harp. Praise him with the timbrel and dance: praise him with stringed instruments and organs. Praise him upon the loud cymbals: praise him upon the high sounding cymbals."—Psalm 150:3–5.

"Serve the LORD with gladness: come before his presence with singing."—Psalm 100:2.

"When the morning stars sang together, and all the sons of God shouted for joy?"—Job 38:7.

"I will sing of mercy and judgment: unto thee, O LORD, will I sing."—Psalm 101:1.

There are hundreds of references in the Bible concerning music. Many of them show us how precious the singing of Christians really is to our Lord. Every beautiful melody is a gift from Him.

"But I have trusted in thy mercy; my heart shall rejoice in thy salvation. I will sing unto the LORD, because he hath dealt bountifully with me."—Psalm 13:5, 6.

"Let the word of Christ dwell in you richly in all wisdom; teaching and admonishing one another in psalms and hymns and spiritual songs, singing with grace in your hearts to the Lord."—Colossians 3:16.

"And he hath put a new song in my mouth, even praise unto our God: many shall see it, and fear, and shall trust in the LORD."—Psalm 40:3.

21

"It came even to pass, as the trumpeters and singers were as one, to make one sound to be heard in praising and thanking the LORD; and when they lifted up their voice with the trumpets and cymbals and instruments of musick, and praised the LORD, saying, For he is good; for his mercy endureth for ever: that then the house was filled with a cloud, even the house of the LORD."—II Chronicles 5:13.

"O come, let us sing unto the LORD: let us make a joyful noise to the rock of our salvation."—Psalm 95:1.

"And at midnight Paul and Silas prayed, and sang praises unto God: and the prisoners heard them."—Acts 16:25.

"Sing unto the LORD with thanksgiving; sing praise upon the harp unto our God."—Psalm 147:7.

"Then was our mouth filled with laughter, and our tongue with singing: then said they among the heathen, The LORD hath done great things for them."—Psalm 126:2.

"The whole earth is at rest, and is quiet: they break forth into singing."—Isaiah 14:7.

"Sing unto him, sing psalms unto him: talk ye of all his wondrous works."—Psalm 105:2.

"Praise ye the LORD: for it is good to sing praises unto our God; for it is pleasant; and praise is comely."—Psalm 147:1.

I learned more about the Bible through music than any other way.

—Mrs. John R. Rice

CHURCH

"Therefore as the church is subject unto Christ, so let the wives be to their own husbands in every thing. Husbands, love your wives, even as Christ also loved the church, and gave himself for it." —Ephesians 5:24, 25.

"Not forsaking the assembling of ourselves together, as the manner of some is; but exhorting one another: and so much the more, as ye see the day approaching." —Hebrews 10:25.

"And I say also unto thee, That thou art Peter, and upon this rock I will build my church; and the gates of hell shall not prevail against it." —Matthew 16:18.

* Jesus loved and gave Himself for the Church.
* Those who have given their hearts and lives to Christ.
* The body of Christ.

"And so were the churches established in the faith, and increased in number daily." —Acts 16:5.

"And he is the head of the body, the church: who is the beginning, the firstborn from the dead; that in all things he might have the preeminence." —Colossians 1:18.

"For as the body is one, and hath many members, and all the members of that one body, being many, are one body: so also is Christ. For by one Spirit are we all baptized into one body, whether we be Jews or Gentiles, whether we be bond or free; and have been all made to drink into one Spirit. For the body is not one member, but many." —I Corinthians 12:12–14.

"And they continued stedfastly in the apostles' doctrine and fellowship, and in breaking of bread, and in prayers." —Acts 2:42.

"Ye also, as lively stones, are built up a spiritual house, an holy priesthood, to offer up spiritual sacrifices, acceptable to God by Jesus Christ."—I Peter 2:5.

"Now therefore ye are no more strangers and foreigners, but fellowcitizens with the saints, and of the household of God; And are built upon the foundation of the apostles and prophets, Jesus Christ himself being the chief corner stone."—Ephesians 2:19,20.

"Praising God, and having favour with all the people. And the Lord added to the church daily such as should be saved."—Acts 2:47.

"Take heed therefore unto yourselves, and to all the flock, over the which the Holy Ghost hath made you overseers, to feed the church of God, which he hath purchased with his own blood."—Acts 20:28.

The early church was:
A believing church
An obedient church
A steadfast church
A praying church
A worshiping church
A joyful church
An effective church
A growing church

—Unknown

COMMITMENT

"Into thine hand I commit my spirit: thou hast redeemed me, O LORD God of truth."—Psalm 31:5.

"So built we the wall; and all the wall was joined together unto the half thereof: for the people had a mind to work."—Nehemiah 4:6.

"And they straightway left their nets, and followed him. And going on from thence, he saw other two brethren, James the son of Zebedee, and John his brother, in a ship with Zebedee their father, mending their nets; and he called them. And they immediately left the ship and their father, and followed him."—Matthew 4:20–22.

A positive effort to faithfully serve Christ according to the guidelines He sets for us in the Bible.

"For whosoever will save his life shall lose it; but whosoever shall lose his life for my sake and the gospel's, the same shall save it."—Mark 8:35.

"I beseech you therefore, brethren, by the mercies of God, that ye present your bodies a living sacrifice, holy, acceptable unto God, which is your reasonable service. And be not conformed to this world: but be ye transformed by the renewing of your mind, that ye may prove what is that good, and acceptable, and perfect, will of God."—Romans 12:1, 2.

"I am crucified with Christ: nevertheless I live; yet not I, but Christ liveth in me: and the life which I now live in the flesh I live by the faith of the Son of God, who loved me, and gave himself for me."—Galatians 2:20.

"This I say then, Walk in the Spirit, and ye shall not fulfil the lust of the flesh."—Galatians 5:16.

"Commit thy way unto the LORD; trust also in him; and he shall bring it to pass."—Psalm 37:5.

"O Timothy, keep that which is committed to thy trust, avoiding profane and vain babblings, and oppositions of science falsely so called."—I Timothy 6:20.

"Now thanks be unto God, which always causeth us to triumph in Christ, and maketh manifest the savour of his knowledge by us in every place."—II Corinthians 2:14.

"Now therefore fear the LORD, and serve him in sincerity and in truth: and put away the gods which your fathers served on the other side of the flood, and in Egypt; and serve ye the LORD."—Joshua 24:14.

"No man can serve two masters: for either he will hate the one, and love the other; or else he will hold to the one, and despise the other. Ye cannot serve God and mammon."—Matthew 6:24.

Every divine promise is built upon four pillars: God's justice or holiness, which will not suffer Him to deceive; His grace or goodness, which will not suffer Him to forget; His truth, which will not suffer Him to change; and His power, which makes Him able to accomplish.

—Salter

(With such a wonderful Heavenly Father, how can we not be totally committed to Him?)

COMPLAINING

"I said, I will take heed to my ways, that I sin not with my tongue: I will keep my mouth with a bridle, while the wicked is before me."—Psalm 39:1.

"Do all things without murmurings and disputings: That ye may be blameless and harmless, the sons of God, without rebuke, in the midst of a crooked and perverse nation, among whom ye shine as lights in the world."—Philippians 2:14, 15.

"Jesus therefore answered and said unto them, Murmur not among yourselves."—John 6:43.

"Nay but, O man, who art thou that repliest against God? Shall the thing formed say to him that formed it, Why hast thou made me thus?"—Romans 9:20.

"Where is the wise? where is the scribe? where is the disputer of this world? hath not God made foolish the wisdom of this world?"—I Corinthians 1:20.

Instead of accepting God's Word and His sovereign will, we often are guilty of expressing our dissatisfaction with what is happening in our lives and in the lives of others around us. Often the problems are of our own making.

"But avoid foolish questions, and genealogies, and contentions, and strivings about the law; for they are unprofitable and vain."—Titus 3:9.

"Therefore I will not refrain my mouth; I will speak in the anguish of my spirit; I will complain in the bitterness of my soul."—Job 7:11.

"But Martha was cumbered about much serving, and came to him, and said, Lord, dost thou not care that my sister hath left me to serve alone? bid her therefore that she help me. And Jesus answered and said unto her, Martha, Martha, thou art careful and troubled about many things: But one thing is needful: and Mary hath chosen that good part, which shall not be taken away from her."—Luke 10:40–42.

"And when the people complained, it displeased the LORD: *and the* LORD *heard it; and his anger was kindled; and the fire of the* LORD *burnt among them, and consumed them that were in the uttermost parts of the camp."*— Numbers 11:1.

"Even to day is my complaint bitter: my stroke is heavier than my groaning."—Job 23:2.

"I poured out my complaint before him; I shewed before him my trouble."—Psalm 142:2.

"Speak not evil one of another, brethren. He that speaketh evil of his brother, and judgeth his brother, speaketh evil of the law, and judgeth the law: but if thou judge the law, thou art not a doer of the law, but a judge."—James 4:11.

"Let no corrupt communication proceed out of your mouth, but that which is good to the use of edifying, that it may minister grace unto the hearers."—Ephesians 4:29.

When I complain, I do it because "it's good to get things off my chest." When you complain, I remind you that "griping doesn't help anything."

–Sidney Harris

CONSCIENCE

"That which we have seen and heard declare we unto you, that ye also may have fellowship with us: and truly our fellowship is with the Father, and with his Son Jesus Christ. And these things write we unto you, that your joy may be full. This then is the message which we have heard of him, and declare unto you, that God is light, and in him is no darkness at all. If we say that we have fellowship with him, and walk in darkness, we lie, and do not the truth: But if we walk in the light, as he is in the light, we have fellowship one with another, and the blood of Jesus Christ his Son cleanseth us from all sin. If we say that we have no sin, we deceive ourselves, and the truth is not in us. If we confess our sins, he is faithful and just to forgive us our sins, and to cleanse us from all unrighteousness. If we say that we have not sinned, we make him a liar, and his word is not in us."—I John 1:3–10.

"Thou wilt keep him in perfect peace, whose mind is stayed on thee: because he trusteth in thee."—Isaiah 26:3.

A clear conscience is one of life's most prized possessions.

"But now in Christ Jesus ye who sometimes were far off are made nigh by the blood of Christ. For he is our peace, who hath made both one, and hath broken down the middle wall of partition between us."—Ephesians 2:13, 14.

"He that saith he is in the light, and hateth his brother, is in darkness even until now. He that loveth his brother abideth in the light, and there is none occasion of stumbling in him. But he that hateth his brother is in darkness, and walketh in darkness, and knoweth not whither he goeth, because that darkness hath blinded his eyes."—I John 2:9–11.

NEVER QUIT!

"But without faith it is impossible to please him: for he that cometh to God must believe that he is, and that he is a rewarder of them that diligently seek him."—Hebrews 11:6.

"Be careful for nothing; but in every thing by prayer and supplication with thanksgiving let your requests be made known unto God. And the peace of God, which passeth all understanding, shall keep your hearts and minds through Christ Jesus. Finally, brethren, whatsoever things are true, whatsoever things are honest, whatsoever things are just, whatsoever things are pure, whatsoever things are lovely, whatsoever things are of good report; if there be any virtue, and if there be any praise, think on these things. Those things, which ye have both learned, and received, and heard, and seen in me, do: and the God of peace shall be with you."—Philippians 4:6–9.

"That ye might walk worthy of the Lord unto all pleasing, being fruitful in every good work, and increasing in the knowledge of God."—Colossians 1:10.

"I acknowledged my sin unto thee, and mine iniquity have I not hid. I said, I will confess my transgressions unto the LORD; and thou forgavest the iniquity of my sin. Selah."—Psalm 32:5.

"He that covereth his sins shall not prosper: but whoso confesseth and forsaketh them shall have mercy."—Proverbs 28:13.

"Confess your faults one to another, and pray one for another, that ye may be healed. The effectual fervent prayer of a righteous man availeth much."—James 5:16.

When a man says he has a clear conscience, it often means he has a bad memory.

–Unknown

COURAGE

"I can do all things through Christ which strengtheneth me."—Philippians 4:13.

"Let us therefore come boldly unto the throne of grace, that we may obtain mercy, and find grace to help in time of need."—Hebrews 4:16.

*"Be strong and of a good courage, fear not, nor be afraid of them: for the L*ORD *thy God, he it is that doth go with thee; he will not fail thee, nor forsake thee."*—Deuteronomy 31:6.

Courage may be defined as the facing of a problem or difficulty, with godly resolve, never minding the cost or the fear.

*"Only be thou strong and very courageous, that thou mayest observe to do according to all the law, which Moses my servant commanded thee: turn not from it to the right hand or to the left, that thou mayest prosper whithersoever thou goest. This book of the law shall not depart out of thy mouth; but thou shalt meditate therein day and night, that thou mayest observe to do according to all that is written therein: for then thou shalt make thy way prosperous, and then thou shalt have good success. Have not I commanded thee? Be strong and of a good courage; be not afraid, neither be thou dismayed: for the L*ORD *thy God is with thee whithersoever thou goest."*—Joshua 1:7–9.

"Finally, my brethren, be strong in the Lord, and in the power of his might. Put on the whole armour of God, that ye may be able to stand against the wiles of the devil. For we wrestle not against flesh and blood, but against principalities, against powers, against the rulers of the darkness of this world, against spiritual wickedness in high places."—Ephesians 6:10–12.

NEVER QUIT!

"If thou faint in the day of adversity, thy strength is small."—Proverbs 24:10.

"Fear thou not; for I am with thee: be not dismayed; for I am thy God: I will strengthen thee; yea, I will help thee; yea, I will uphold thee with the right hand of my righteousness."—Isaiah 41:10.

"Only let your conversation be as it becometh the gospel of Christ: that whether I come and see you, or else be absent, I may hear of your affairs, that ye stand fast in one spirit, with one mind striving together for the faith of the gospel; And in nothing terrified by your adversaries: which is to them an evident token of perdition, but to you of salvation, and that of God. For unto you it is given in the behalf of Christ, not only to believe on him, but also to suffer for his sake."—Philippians 1:27–29.

"And from thence, when the brethren heard of us, they came to meet us as far as Appii forum, and The three taverns: whom when Paul saw, he thanked God, and took courage."—Acts 28:15.

"Go, gather together all the Jews that are present in Shushan, and fast ye for me, and neither eat nor drink three days, night or day: I also and my maidens will fast likewise; and so will I go in unto the king, which is not according to the law: and if I perish, I perish."—Esther 4:16.

You cannot run away from a weakness; you must sometimes fight it out or perish. And if that be so, why not now, and where you stand?

–Robert L. Stevenson

COURTING

"Wherewithal shall a young man cleanse his way? by taking heed thereto according to thy word. With my whole heart have I sought thee: O let me not wander from thy commandments. Thy word have I hid in mine heart, that I might not sin against thee."—Psalm 119:9–11.

"Even a child is known by his doings, whether his work be pure, and whether it be right."—Proverbs 20:11.

"Be not deceived: evil communications corrupt good manners."—I Corinthians 15:33.

"Be ye not unequally yoked together with unbelievers: for what fellowship hath righteousness with unrighteousness? and what communion hath light with darkness?"—II Corinthians 6:14.

"The integrity of the upright shall guide them: but the perverseness of transgressors shall destroy them."—Proverbs 11:3.

The right kind of dating is very important for Christians because testimonies are at stake. You will become like the people with whom you associate on a regular basis.

"Let no man despise thy youth; but be thou an example of the believers, in word, in conversation, in charity, in spirit, in faith, in purity."—I Timothy 4:12.

"Nevertheless he that standeth stedfast in his heart, having no necessity, but hath power over his own will, and hath so decreed in his heart that he will keep his virgin, doeth well."—I Corinthians 7:37.

33

"And walk in love, as Christ also hath loved us, and hath given himself for us an offering and a sacrifice to God for a sweetsmelling savour. But fornication, and all uncleanness, or covetousness, let it not be once named among you, as becometh saints."—Ephesians 5:2,3.

"Rejoice, O young man, in thy youth; and let thy heart cheer thee in the days of thy youth, and walk in the ways of thine heart, and in the sight of thine eyes: but know thou, that for all these things God will bring thee into judgment."—Ecclesiastes 11:9.

"Remember now thy Creator in the days of thy youth, while the evil days come not, nor the years draw nigh, when thou shalt say, I have no pleasure in them."—Ecclesiastes 12:1.

"And whatsoever ye do in word or deed, do all in the name of the Lord Jesus, giving thanks to God and the Father by him."—Colossians 3:17.

"Delight thyself also in the LORD; and he shall give thee the desires of thine heart."—Psalm 37:4.

"Trust in the LORD with all thine heart; and lean not unto thine own understanding. In all thy ways acknowledge him, and he shall direct thy paths."—Proverbs 3:5,6.

Courtship is when a young man gets tripped by a girl who's putting her best foot forward.

—Franklin P. Jones

DEATH

"Precious in the sight of the LORD is the death of his saints."—Psalm 116:15.

"For since by man came death, by man came also the resurrection of the dead. For as in Adam all die, even so in Christ shall all be made alive."—I Corinthians 15:21, 22.

"As righteousness tendeth to life: so he that pursueth evil pursueth it to his own death."—Proverbs 11:19.

"Yea, though I walk through the valley of the shadow of death, I will fear no evil: for thou art with me; thy rod and thy staff they comfort me."—Psalm 23:4.

"Wherefore, as by one man sin entered into the world, and death by sin; and so death passed upon all men, for that all have sinned."—Romans 5:12.

Death marks the end of life on this earth and the beginning of life with our Heavenly Father.

"In the way of righteousness is life; and in the pathway thereof there is no death."—Proverbs 12:28.

"And as it is appointed unto men once to die, but after this the judgment: So Christ was once offered to bear the sins of many; and unto them that look for him shall he appear the second time without sin unto salvation."—Hebrews 9:27, 28.

"For whoso findeth me findeth life, and shall obtain favour of the LORD. But he that sinneth against me wrongeth his own soul: all they that hate me love death."—Proverbs 8:35, 36.

"For if we believe that Jesus died and rose again, even so them also which sleep in Jesus will God bring with him."— I Thessalonians 4:14.

"Beloved, now are we the sons of God, and it doth not yet appear what we shall be: but we know that, when he shall appear, we shall be like him; for we shall see him as he is."— I John 3:2.

"The last enemy that shall be destroyed is death."— I Corinthians 15:26.

"And God shall wipe away all tears from their eyes; and there shall be no more death, neither sorrow, nor crying, neither shall there be any more pain: for the former things are passed away."—Revelation 21:4.

"O death, where is thy sting? O grave, where is thy victory? The sting of death is sin; and the strength of sin is the law. But thanks be to God, which giveth us the victory through our Lord Jesus Christ."—I Corinthians 15:55–57.

If Christ is your Saviour, you are as sure of Heaven as if you were there right now.

–Lee Roberson

DEVOTIONS

"We love him, because he first loved us."—I John 4:19.

"O God, thou art my God; early will I seek thee: my soul thirsteth for thee, my flesh longeth for thee in a dry and thirsty land, where no water is."—Psalm 63:1.

Spending time in God's Word and in prayer, in response to His great love for us. Some call it a "quiet time."

"And he read therein before the street that was before the water gate from the morning until midday, before the men and the women, and those that could understand; and the ears of all the people were attentive unto the book of the law."—Nehemiah 8:3.

"But we all, with open face beholding as in a glass the glory of the Lord, are changed into the same image from glory to glory, even as by the Spirit of the Lord."—II Corinthians 3:18.

"Mine eyes prevent the night watches, that I might meditate in thy word."—Psalm 119:148.

"But his delight is in the law of the LORD; and in his law doth he meditate day and night."—Psalm 1:2.

"But they that wait upon the LORD shall renew their strength; they shall mount up with wings as eagles; they shall run, and not be weary; and they shall walk, and not faint."—Isaiah 40:31.

"And the LORD appeared again in Shiloh: for the LORD revealed himself to Samuel in Shiloh by the word of the LORD."—I Samuel 3:21.

"Now when Daniel knew that the writing was signed, he went into his house; and his windows being open in his chamber toward Jerusalem, he kneeled upon his knees three times a day, and prayed, and gave thanks before his God, as he did aforetime."—Daniel 6:10.

"Thy words were found, and I did eat them; and thy word was unto me the joy and rejoicing of mine heart: for I am called by thy name, O Lord God of hosts."—Jeremiah 15:16.

"And that from a child thou hast known the holy scriptures, which are able to make thee wise unto salvation through faith which is in Christ Jesus. All scripture is given by inspiration of God, and is profitable for doctrine, for reproof, for correction, for instruction in righteousness."—II Timothy 3:15, 16.

"Study to shew thyself approved unto God, a workman that needeth not to be ashamed, rightly dividing the word of truth."—II Timothy 2:15.

"And in the morning, rising up a great while before day, he went out, and departed into a solitary place, and there prayed."—Mark 1:35.

Devotions are a matter of our heart more than a discipline of our daytimer.

–Dennis Fisher

DOUBT

"And immediately Jesus stretched forth his hand, and caught him, and said unto him, O thou of little faith, wherefore didst thou doubt?"—Matthew 14:31.

"But if thine eye be evil, thy whole body shall be full of darkness. If therefore the light that is in thee be darkness, how great is that darkness!"—Matthew 6:23.

"Behold, the LORD *thy God hath set the land before thee: go up and possess it, as the* LORD *God of thy fathers hath said unto thee; fear not, neither be discouraged."*—Deuteronomy 1:21.

Doubts about the promises and proclamations of the Bible are
troublesome. If entertained too often, they may establish
a dark stopover on the way to the land of disbelief.
They must be confessed and given over
to the Heavenly Father.

"And Gideon said unto him, Oh my Lord, if the LORD *be with us, why then is all this befallen us? and where be all his miracles which our fathers told us of, saying, Did not the* LORD *bring us up from Egypt? but now the* LORD *hath forsaken us, and delivered us into the hands of the Midianites."*—Judges 6:13.

"And he brought him forth abroad, and said, Look now toward heaven, and tell the stars, if thou be able to number them: and he said unto him, So shall thy seed be. And he believed in the LORD; *and he counted it to him for righteousness."*—Genesis 15:5,6.

"For what if some did not believe? shall their unbelief make the faith of God without effect?"—Romans 3:3.

"Jesus said unto him, If thou canst believe, all things are possible to him that believeth. And straightway the father of the child cried out, and said with tears, Lord, I believe; help thou mine unbelief."—Mark 9:23,24.

"Therefore let all the house of Israel know assuredly, that God hath made that same Jesus, whom ye have crucified, both Lord and Christ."—Acts 2:36.

"Now faith is the substance of things hoped for, the evidence of things not seen."—Hebrews 11:1.

"Jesus answered and said unto them, Verily I say unto you, If ye have faith, and doubt not, ye shall not only do this which is done to the fig tree, but also if ye shall say unto this mountain, Be thou removed, and be thou cast into the sea; it shall be done."—Matthew 21:21.

"I am crucified with Christ: nevertheless I live; yet not I, but Christ liveth in me: and the life which I now live in the flesh I live by the faith of the Son of God, who loved me, and gave himself for me."—Galatians 2:20.

"For verily I say unto you, That whosoever shall say unto this mountain, Be thou removed, and be thou cast into the sea; and shall not doubt in his heart, but shall believe that those things which he saith shall come to pass; he shall have whatsoever he saith."—Mark 11:23.

The only cure for the problem of doubt is a sincere study of God's Word on the subjects that give birth to the doubts.

–Lindsay Terry

DRESS

"The woman shall not wear that which pertaineth unto a man, neither shall a man put on a woman's garment: for all that do so are abomination unto the LORD thy God."—Deuteronomy 22:5.

"In like manner also, that women adorn themselves in modest apparel, with shamefacedness and sobriety; not with broided hair, or gold, or pearls, or costly array; But (which becometh women professing godliness) with good works."—I Timothy 2:9,10.

"And he said unto his disciples, Therefore, I say unto you, Take no thought for your life, what ye shall eat; neither for the body, what ye shall put on. The life is more than meat, and the body is more than raiment."—Luke 12:22,23.

The Bible has a great deal to say about what we wear; the coverings that God instituted in the Garden of Eden.

"For we brought nothing into this world, and it is certain we can carry nothing out. And having food and raiment let us be therewith content."—I Timothy 6:7,8.

"Whose adorning let it not be that outward adorning of plaiting the hair, and of wearing of gold, or of putting on of apparel; But let it be the hidden man of the heart, in that which is not corruptible, even the ornament of a meek and quiet spirit, which is in the sight of God of great price."—I Peter 3:3,4.

"She is not afraid of the snow for her household: for all her household are clothed with scarlet."—Proverbs 31:21.

41

"And the seven angels came out of the temple, having the seven plagues, clothed in pure and white linen, and having their breasts girded with golden girdles."—Revelation 15:6.

"I have coveted no man's silver, or gold, or apparel."—Acts 20:33.

"For if there come unto your assembly a man with a gold ring, in goodly apparel, and there come in also a poor man in vile raiment; And ye have respect to him that weareth the gay clothing, and say unto him, Sit thou here in a good place; and say to the poor, Stand thou there, or sit here under my footstool: Are ye not then partial in yourselves, and are become judges of evil thoughts?"—James 2:2–4.

"And when they had mocked him, they took off the purple from him, and put his own clothes on him, and led him out to crucify him."—Mark 15:20.

"Can a man take fire in his bosom, and his clothes not be burned?"—Proverbs 6:27.

"And they come to Jesus, and see him that was possessed with the devil, and had the legion, sitting, and clothed, and in his right mind: and they were afraid."—Mark 5:15.

"But as for me, when they were sick, my clothing was sackcloth: I humbled my soul with fasting; and my prayer returned into mine own bosom."—Psalm 35:13.

**People seldom notice old clothes
if you wear a big smile.**
—Lee Mildon

DRINKING

"And be not drunk with wine, wherein is excess; but be filled with the Spirit; Speaking to yourselves in psalms and hymns and spiritual songs, singing and making melody in your heart to the Lord."—Ephesians 5:18,19.

"Wine is a mocker, strong drink is raging: and whosoever is deceived thereby is not wise."—Proverbs 20:1.

"Envyings, murders, drunkenness, revellings, and such like: of the which I tell you before, as I have also told you in time past, that they which do such things shall not inherit the kingdom of God."—Galatians 5:21.

Alcohol has caused more disaster in the world than
all of the other drugs combined—more death,
more anguish and more hunger.

"Know ye not that the unrighteous shall not inherit the kingdom of God? Be not deceived: neither fornicators, nor idolaters, nor adulterers, nor effeminate, nor abusers of themselves with mankind, Nor thieves, nor covetous, nor drunkards, nor revilers, nor extortioners, shall inherit the kingdom of God."—I Corinthians 6:9,10.

"I beseech you therefore, brethren, by the mercies of God, that ye present your bodies a living sacrifice, holy, acceptable unto God, which is your reasonable service. And be not conformed to this world: but be ye transformed by the renewing of your mind, that ye may prove what is that good, and acceptable, and perfect, will of God."—Romans 12:1,2.

"And take heed to yourselves, lest at any time your hearts be overcharged with surfeiting, and drunkenness, and cares of this life, and so that day come upon you unawares."—Luke 21:34.

"Woe unto them that rise up early in the morning, that they may follow strong drink; that continue until night, till wine inflame them!"—Isaiah 5:11.

"Who hath woe? who hath sorrow? who hath contentions? who hath babbling? who hath wounds without cause? who hath redness of eyes? They that tarry long at the wine; they that go to seek mixed wine."—Proverbs 23:29,30.

"He that loveth pleasure shall be a poor man: he that loveth wine and oil shall not be rich."—Proverbs 21:17.

"It is good neither to eat flesh, nor to drink wine, nor any thing whereby thy brother stumbleth, or is offended, or is made weak."—Romans 14:21.

"For they that sleep sleep in the night; and they that be drunken are drunken in the night. But let us, who are of the day, be sober, putting on the breastplate of faith and love; and for an helmet, the hope of salvation."—I Thessalonians 5:7,8.

A man who drinks now and then usually drinks more now than he did then.

—Unknown

ESTEEM

"The fear of the LORD is the instruction of wisdom; and before honour is humility."—Proverbs 15:33.

"Before destruction the heart of man is haughty, and before honour is humility."—Proverbs 18:12.

"That every one of you should know how to possess his vessel in sanctification and honour."—I Thessalonians 4:4.

"Get wisdom, get understanding: forget it not; neither decline from the words of my mouth....Exalt her, and she shall promote thee: she shall bring thee to honour, when thou dost embrace her."—Proverbs 4:5,8.

"And ye will not come to me, that ye might have life. I receive not honour from men."—John 5:40,41.

"And they were offended in him. But Jesus said unto them, A prophet is not without honour, save in his own country, and in his own house."—Matthew 13:57.

That quality of life that allows one to live with himself without disdain. The reward of true integrity.

"Render therefore to all their dues: tribute to whom tribute is due; custom to whom custom; fear to whom fear; honour to whom honour."—Romans 13:7.

"To execute upon them the judgment written: this honour have all his saints. Praise ye the LORD."—Psalm 149:9.

"He that followeth after righteousness and mercy findeth life, righteousness, and honour."—Proverbs 21:21.

"But glory, honour, and peace, to every man that worketh good, to the Jew first, and also to the Gentile."—Romans 2:10.

"As snow in summer, and as rain in harvest, so honour is not seemly for a fool."—Proverbs 26:1.

"A man's pride shall bring him low: but honour shall uphold the humble in spirit."—Proverbs 29:23.

"And no man taketh this honour unto himself, but he that is called of God, as was Aaron."—Hebrews 5:4.

"Jesus answered, If I honour myself, my honour is nothing: it is my Father that honoureth me; of whom ye say, that he is your God."—John 8:54.

"Strength and honour are her clothing; and she shall rejoice in time to come."—Proverbs 31:25.

The crowning work of all God's matchless
creation is a being from His own hand
into whom He has breathed the breath
of His own life, and who has become
a living soul in His image.

—Joe Henry Hankins

EVIL HABITS

"Thy word have I hid in mine heart, that I might not sin against thee."—Psalm 119:11.

"But shun profane and vain babblings: for they will increase unto more ungodliness."—II Timothy 2:16.

"Abstain from all appearance of evil."—I Thessalonians 5:22.

Evil habits are learned behavior patterns that are counterproductive to a happy Christian existence.

"Having your conversation honest among the Gentiles: that, whereas they speak against you as evildoers, they may by your good works, which they shall behold, glorify God in the day of visitation."—I Peter 2:12.

"Do all things without murmurings and disputings: That ye may be blameless and harmless, the sons of God, without rebuke, in the midst of a crooked and perverse nation, among whom ye shine as lights in the world."—Philippians 2:14, 15.

"Now we command you, brethren, in the name of our Lord Jesus Christ, that ye withdraw yourselves from every brother that walketh disorderly, and not after the tradition which he received of us."—II Thessalonians 3:6.

"For this is the will of God, even your sanctification, that ye should abstain from fornication: That every one of you should know how to possess his vessel in sanctification and honour."—I Thessalonians 4:3, 4.

"Let no man despise thy youth; but be thou an example of the believers, in word, in conversation, in charity, in spirit, in faith, in purity."—I Timothy 4:12.

"Submit yourselves therefore to God. Resist the devil, and he will flee from you."—James 4:7.

"Now the works of the flesh are manifest, which are these; Adultery, fornication, uncleanness, lasciviousness, Idolatry, witchcraft, hatred, variance, emulations, wrath, strife, seditions, heresies, Envyings, murders, drunkenness, revellings, and such like: of the which I tell you before, as I have also told you in time past, that they which do such things shall not inherit the kingdom of God."—Galatians 5:19–21.

"The lip of truth shall be established for ever: but a lying tongue is but for a moment. Deceit is in the heart of them that imagine evil: but to the counsellors of peace is joy. There shall no evil happen to the just: but the wicked shall be filled with mischief. Lying lips are abomination to the LORD: but they that deal truly are his delight."—Proverbs 12:19–22.

"Create in me a clean heart, O God; and renew a right spirit within me."—Psalm 51:10.

The undisciplined is a headache to himself and a heartache to others, and is ill prepared to face the stern realities of life.

–Unknown

FAITH

"Whom having not seen, ye love; in whom, though now ye see him not, yet believing, ye rejoice with joy unspeakable and full of glory: Receiving the end of your faith, even the salvation of your souls."—I Peter 1:8,9.

"But without faith it is impossible to please him: for he that cometh to God must believe that he is, and that he is a rewarder of them that diligently seek him."—Hebrews 11:6.

"For unto us was the gospel preached, as well as unto them: but the word preached did not profit them, not being mixed with faith in them that heard it."—Hebrews 4:2.

"For whatsoever is born of God overcometh the world: and this is the victory that overcometh the world, even our faith."—I John 5:4.

"Now he that hath wrought us for the selfsame thing is God, who also hath given unto us the earnest of the Spirit. Therefore we are always confident, knowing that, whilst we are at home in the body, we are absent from the Lord: (For we walk by faith, not by sight:)."—II Corinthians 5:5–7.

"For in Jesus Christ neither circumcision availeth any thing, nor uncircumcision; but faith which worketh by love."—Galatians 5:6.

It is impossible to please our Heavenly Father apart from faith in Him. Happiness comes to all of God's children who live in such a manner as to please Him.

"Who are kept by the power of God through faith unto salvation ready to be revealed in the last time."—I Peter 1:5.

"Knowing that a man is not justified by the works of the law, but by the faith of Jesus Christ, even we have believed in Jesus Christ, that we might be justified by the faith of Christ, and not by the works of the law: for by the works of the law shall no flesh be justified."—Galatians 2:16.

"Wherefore the law was our schoolmaster to bring us unto Christ, that we might be justified by faith."—Galatians 3:24.

"Therefore being justified by faith, we have peace with God through our Lord Jesus Christ."—Romans 5:1.

"For by grace are ye saved through faith; and that not of yourselves: it is the gift of God: Not of works, lest any man should boast."—Ephesians 2:8,9.

"Watch ye, stand fast in the faith, quit you like men, be strong."—I Corinthians 16:13.

"For though I be absent in the flesh, yet am I with you in the spirit, joying and beholding your order, and the stedfastness of your faith in Christ."—Colossians 2:5.

"Now faith is the substance of things hoped for, the evidence of things not seen."—Hebrews 11:1.

"So then faith cometh by hearing, and hearing by the word of God."—Romans 10:17.

"And Jesus answering saith unto them, Have faith in God."—Mark 11:22.

You are not alone, my Christian friend. You are not alone when you have faith in Jesus Christ. You can rest upon Him and know He is with you in this and every hour.

—Lee Roberson

FAMILY/HOME

"And if it seem evil unto you to serve the LORD, choose you this day whom ye will serve; whether the gods which your fathers served that were on the other side of the flood, or the gods of the Amorites, in whose land ye dwell: but as for me and my house, we will serve the LORD."—Joshua 24:15.

"And he shall turn the heart of the fathers to the children, and the heart of the children to their fathers, lest I come and smite the earth with a curse."—Malachi 4:6.

"Better is a dry morsel, and quietness therewith, than an house full of sacrifices with strife."—Proverbs 17:1.

**We build a house with our hands and
a home with our hearts.**

—Lindsay Terry

"Children, obey your parents in the Lord: for this is right. Honour thy father and mother; (which is the first commandment with promise;) That it may be well with thee, and thou mayest live long on the earth. And, ye fathers, provoke not your children to wrath: but bring them up in the nurture and admonition of the Lord."—Ephesians 6:1–4.

"And these words, which I command thee this day, shall be in thine heart: And thou shalt teach them diligently unto thy children, and shalt talk of them when thou sittest in thine house, and when thou walkest by the way, and when thou liest down, and when thou risest up."—Deuteronomy 6:6,7.

"Train up a child in the way he should go: and when he is old, he will not depart from it."—Proverbs 22:6.

"Honour thy father and thy mother: that thy days may be long upon the land which the LORD thy God giveth thee."— Exodus 20:12.

"Lo, children are an heritage of the LORD: and the fruit of the womb is his reward. As arrows are in the hand of a mighty man; so are children of the youth."— Psalm 127:3, 4.

"Children's children are the crown of old men; and the glory of children are their fathers."— Proverbs 17:6.

"But if any widow have children or nephews, let them learn first to shew piety at home, and to requite their parents: for that is good and acceptable before God."— I Timothy 5:4.

"To be discreet, chaste, keepers at home, good, obedient to their own husbands, that the word of God be not blasphemed."— Titus 2:5.

The family is the basic unit of society; and long before the founding of the church, the organization of government or the establishment of a school or a business, God put the family together.

—Raymond Barber

A broken home is the world's greatest wreck.

—Unknown

FEAR

"And he said unto them, Why are ye so fearful? how is it that ye have no faith?"—Mark 4:40.

"For God hath not given us the spirit of fear; but of power, and of love, and of a sound mind."—II Timothy 1:7.

"Happy is the man that feareth alway: but he that hardeneth his heart shall fall into mischief."—Proverbs 28:14.

"Say to them that are of a fearful heart, Be strong, fear not: behold, your God will come with vengeance, even God with a recompence; he will come and save you."—Isaiah 35:4.

"I sought the LORD, and he heard me, and delivered me from all my fears."—Psalm 34:4.

Fear is often a monstrous enemy to Christians. And yet, there are two kinds—a healthy fear and a debilitating fear.

"Fear not, little flock; for it is your Father's good pleasure to give you the kingdom."—Luke 12:32.

"They that fear thee will be glad when they see me; because I have hoped in thy word."—Psalm 119:74.

"For I the LORD thy God will hold thy right hand, saying unto thee, Fear not; I will help thee."—Isaiah 41:13.

"For ye have not received the spirit of bondage again to fear; but ye have received the Spirit of adoption, whereby we cry, Abba, Father."—Romans 8:15.

"Let your conversation be without covetousness; and be content with such things as ye have: for he hath said, I will never leave thee, nor forsake thee. So that we may boldly say, The Lord is my helper, and I will not fear what man shall do unto me."—Hebrews 13:5,6.

"The LORD is on my side; I will not fear: what can man do unto me? The LORD taketh my part with them that help me: therefore shall I see my desire upon them that hate me. It is better to trust in the LORD than to put confidence in man. It is better to trust in the LORD than to put confidence in princes."—Psalm 118:6–9.

"The fear of man bringeth a snare: but whoso putteth his trust in the LORD shall be safe."—Proverbs 29:25.

"Be not afraid of sudden fear, neither of the desolation of the wicked, when it cometh. For the LORD shall be thy confidence, and shall keep thy foot from being taken."—Proverbs 3:25,26.

Fear is more painful to cowards than death is to those who have godly courage.

—Lindsay Terry

FRIENDS

"A froward man soweth strife: and a whisperer separateth chief friends."—Proverbs 16:28.

"Greater love hath no man than this, that a man lay down his life for his friends. Ye are my friends, if ye do whatsoever I command you. Henceforth I call you not servants; for the servant knoweth not what his lord doeth: but I have called you friends; for all things that I have heard of my Father I have made known unto you."—John 15:13–15.

"A friend loveth at all times, and a brother is born for adversity."—Proverbs 17:17.

"A man that hath friends must shew himself friendly: and there is a friend that sticketh closer than a brother."—Proverbs 18:24.

It is unusual for a person to have more than a very few close friends—people who love him, warts and all, and who will in all things be honest with him.

"And the scripture was fulfilled which saith, Abraham believed God, and it was imputed unto him for righteousness: and he was called the Friend of God."—James 2:23.

"He that walketh with wise men shall be wise: but a companion of fools shall be destroyed."—Proverbs 13:20.

"Ye adulterers and adulteresses, know ye not that the friendship of the world is enmity with God? whosoever therefore will be a friend of the world is the enemy of God."—James 4:4.

"Can two walk together, except they be agreed?"—Amos 3:3.

"Bear ye one another's burdens, and so fulfil the law of Christ."—Galatians 6:2.

"Faithful are the wounds of a friend; but the kisses of an enemy are deceitful."—Proverbs 27:6.

"For if they fall, the one will lift up his fellow: but woe to him that is alone when he falleth; for he hath not another to help him up."—Ecclesiastes 4:10.

"Thine own friend, and thy father's friend, forsake not; neither go into thy brother's house in the day of thy calamity: for better is a neighbour that is near than a brother far off."—Proverbs 27:10.

"Finally, be ye all of one mind, having compassion one of another, love as brethren, be pitiful, be courteous: Not rendering evil for evil, or railing for railing: but contrariwise blessing; knowing that ye are thereunto called, that ye should inherit a blessing."—I Peter 3:8,9.

Happy is the man who has a friend.
Happier is the man who is a friend.
Happiest is the man who has a friend
and who is a friend.

—Jack Hyles

GENEROSITY

"Give to him that asketh thee, and from him that would borrow of thee turn not thou away." —Matthew 5:42.

"There is that scattereth, and yet increaseth; and there is that withholdeth more than is meet, but it tendeth to poverty. The liberal soul shall be made fat: and he that watereth shall be watered also himself." —Proverbs 11:24, 25.

"He that is first in his own cause seemeth just; but his neighbour cometh and searcheth him." —Proverbs 18:17.

"He is ever merciful, and lendeth; and his seed is blessed." —Psalm 37:26.

Many a burden has been lifted by the generosity
of a faithful friend or an individual who saw
a need and wanted to meet it.

"Speak unto the children of Israel, that they bring me an offering: of every man that giveth it willingly with his heart ye shall take my offering." —Exodus 25:2.

"The desire of the slothful killeth him; for his hands refuse to labour. He coveteth greedily all the day long: but the righteous giveth and spareth not." —Proverbs 21:25, 26.

"Take heed that ye do not your alms before men, to be seen of them: otherwise ye have no reward of your Father which is in heaven." —Matthew 6:1.

"He that hath a bountiful eye shall be blessed; for he giveth of his bread to the poor." —Proverbs 22:9.

NEVER QUIT!

"But this I say, He which soweth sparingly shall reap also sparingly; and he which soweth bountifully shall reap also bountifully. Every man according as he purposeth in his heart, so let him give; not grudgingly, or of necessity: for God loveth a cheerful giver."—II Corinthians 9:6,7.

"Withhold not good from them to whom it is due, when it is in the power of thine hand to do it."—Proverbs 3:27.

"Therefore, as ye abound in every thing, in faith, and utterance, and knowledge, and in all diligence, and in your love to us, see that ye abound in this grace also."—II Corinthians 8:7.

"How that in a great trial of affliction the abundance of their joy and their deep poverty abounded unto the riches of their liberality."—II Corinthians 8:2.

"And whosoever shall give to drink unto one of these little ones a cup of cold water only in the name of a disciple, verily I say unto you, he shall in no wise lose his reward."—Matthew 10:42.

**You cannot try to be generous.
Either you are, or you ain't.**
—Lindsay Terry

GIFTS OF GOD

"For the wages of sin is death; but the gift of God is eternal life through Jesus Christ our Lord."—Romans 6:23.

"God also bearing them witness, both with signs and wonders, and with divers miracles, and gifts of the Holy Ghost, according to his own will?"—Hebrews 2:4.

"Now there are diversities of gifts, but the same Spirit. And there are differences of administrations, but the same Lord."—I Corinthians 12:4,5.

"And he gave some, apostles; and some, prophets; and some, evangelists; and some, pastors and teachers."—Ephesians 4:11.

"For by grace are ye saved through faith; and that not of yourselves: it is the gift of God."—Ephesians 2:8.

God is more intent on giving to you and me
than we are on getting gifts from Him.

"Jesus answered and said unto her, If thou knewest the gift of God, and who it is that saith to thee, Give me to drink; thou wouldest have asked of him, and he would have given thee living water."—John 4:10.

"If ye then, being evil, know how to give good gifts unto your children: how much more shall your heavenly Father give the Holy Spirit to them that ask him?"—Luke 11:13.

"For I would that all men were even as I myself. But every man hath his proper gift of God, one after this manner, and another after that."—I Corinthians 7:7.

59

"Then Peter said unto them, Repent, and be baptized every one of you in the name of Jesus Christ for the remission of sins, and ye shall receive the gift of the Holy Ghost. For the promise is unto you, and to your children, and to all that are afar off, even as many as the Lord our God shall call."—Acts 2:38,39.

"Having then gifts differing according to the grace that is given to us, whether prophecy, let us prophesy according to the proportion of faith."—Romans 12:6.

"Even so ye, forasmuch as ye are zealous of spiritual gifts, seek that ye may excel to the edifying of the church."—I Corinthians 14:12.

"Wherefore I put thee in remembrance that thou stir up the gift of God, which is in thee by the putting on of my hands."—II Timothy 1:6.

"As every man hath received the gift, even so minister the same one to another, as good stewards of the manifold grace of God."—I Peter 4:10.

"Every good gift and every perfect gift is from above, and cometh down from the Father of lights, with whom is no variableness, neither shadow of turning."—James 1:17.

It is equally easy for God to supply our greatest needs as well as our smallest wants…just as the ocean bears the battleship as easily as the fisherman's vessel.

–Thomas Guthrie

GOD'S GRACE

"I marvel that ye are so soon removed from him that called you into the grace of Christ unto another gospel."—Galatians 1:6.

"Being justified freely by his grace through the redemption that is in Christ Jesus."—Romans 3:24.

"And the Word was made flesh, and dwelt among us, (and we beheld his glory, the glory as of the only begotten of the Father,) full of grace and truth."—John 1:14.

"For by grace are ye saved through faith; and that not of yourselves: it is the gift of God: Not of works, lest any man should boast."—Ephesians 2:8,9.

Unearned and undeserved favor
from our Heavenly Father.

"Grace be with all them that love our Lord Jesus Christ in sincerity. Amen."—Ephesians 6:24.

"But he giveth more grace. Wherefore he saith, God resisteth the proud, but giveth grace unto the humble."—James 4:6.

"And of his fulness have all we received, and grace for grace. For the law was given by Moses, but grace and truth came by Jesus Christ."—John 1:16,17.

"And he said unto me, My grace is sufficient for thee: for my strength is made perfect in weakness. Most gladly therefore will I rather glory in my infirmities, that the power of Christ may rest upon me."—II Corinthians 12:9.

"For the LORD God is a sun and shield: the LORD will give grace and glory: no good thing will he withhold from them that walk uprightly."—Psalm 84:11.

"For ye know the grace of our Lord Jesus Christ, that, though he was rich, yet for your sakes he became poor, that ye through his poverty might be rich."—II Corinthians 8:9.

"But grow in grace, and in the knowledge of our Lord and Saviour Jesus Christ. To him be glory both now and for ever. Amen."—II Peter 3:18.

"And with great power gave the apostles witness of the resurrection of the Lord Jesus: and great grace was upon them all."—Acts 4:33.

Manifold grace means that it is not just one blessing, but there are thousands to come, one after another. The joy you have multiplies the joys to come; the victory you have in Christ multiplies the coming conquests.

–Paul Rader

GOD'S WORD

"Thy word is true from the beginning: and every one of thy righteous judgments endureth for ever."—Psalm 119:160.

"Forever, O LORD, thy word is settled in heaven."—Psalm 119:89.

"And that from a child thou hast known the holy scriptures, which are able to make thee wise unto salvation through faith which is in Christ Jesus. All scripture is given by inspiration of God, and is profitable for doctrine, for reproof, for correction, for instruction in righteousness."—II Timothy 3:15, 16.

"The grass withereth, the flower fadeth: but the word of our God shall stand for ever."—Isaiah 40:8.

"Concerning thy testimonies, I have known of old that Thou hast founded them for ever."—Psalm 119:152.

The verbally inspired, eternal, inerrant
Word of God. The guide for our lives

"The law of the LORD is perfect, converting the soul: the testimony of the LORD is sure, making wise the simple."—Psalm 19:7.

"Being born again, not of corruptible seed, but of incorruptible, by the word of God, which liveth and abideth for ever. For all flesh is as grass, and all the glory of man as the flower of grass. The grass withereth, and the flower thereof falleth away: But the word of the Lord endureth for ever. And this is the word which by the gospel is preached unto you."—I Peter 1:23–25.

"For the prophecy came not in old time by the will of man: but holy men of God spake as they were moved by the Holy Ghost."—II Peter 1:21.

"Every word of God is pure: he is a shield unto them that put their trust in him."—Proverbs 30:5.

"But he answered and said, It is written, Man shall not live by bread alone, but by every word that proceedeth out of the mouth of God."—Matthew 4:4.

"For the word of God is quick, and powerful, and sharper than any twoedged sword, piercing even to the dividing asunder of soul and spirit, and of the joints and marrow, and is a discerner of the thoughts and intents of the heart."—Hebrews 4:12.

"Thy word have I hid in mine heart, that I might not sin against thee."—Psalm 119:11.

"Study to shew thyself approved unto God, a workman that needeth not to be ashamed, rightly dividing the word of truth."—II Timothy 2:15.

"Which things also we speak, not in the words which man's wisdom teacheth, but which the Holy Ghost teacheth; comparing spiritual things with spiritual."—I Corinthians 2:13.

Nothing any man can say or think about the Bible is as important as what the Bible says about itself.

—John R. Rice

GRIEVING

"Blessed are they that mourn: for they shall be comforted."—Matthew 5:4.

"For we know that if our earthly house of this tabernacle were dissolved, we have a building of God, an house not made with hands, eternal in the heavens."—II Corinthians 5:1.

"Let not your heart be troubled: ye believe in God, believe also in me."—John 14:1.

"It is of the LORD'S mercies that we are not consumed, because his compassions fail not. They are new every morning: great is thy faithfulness."—Lamentations 3:22,23.

A time of mourning that God allows His children to pass through. However, it is not as those who have no hope.

"Blessed be the God and Father of our Lord Jesus Christ, which according to his abundant mercy hath begotten us again unto a lively hope by the resurrection of Jesus Christ from the dead, To an inheritance incorruptible, and undefiled, and that fadeth not away, reserved in heaven for you, Who are kept by the power of God through faith unto salvation ready to be revealed in the last time."—I Peter 1:3–5.

"But I would not have you to be ignorant, brethren, concerning them which are asleep, that ye sorrow not, even as others which have no hope. For if we believe that Jesus died and rose again, even so them also which sleep in Jesus will God bring with him."—I Thessalonians 4:13,14.

"Is there no balm in Gilead; is there no physician there? why then is not the health of the daughter of my people recovered?"—Jeremiah 8:22.

Never Quit!

"I thank God, whom I serve from my forefathers with pure conscience, that without ceasing I have remembrance of thee in my prayers night and day; Greatly desiring to see thee, being mindful of thy tears, that I may be filled with joy."—II Timothy 1:3,4.

"And when the Lord saw her, he had compassion on her, and said unto her, Weep not."—Luke 7:13.

"These things I have spoken unto you, that in me ye might have peace. In the world ye shall have tribulation: but be of good cheer; I have overcome the world."—John 16:33.

"Now the Lord of peace himself give you peace always by all means. The Lord be with you all."—II Thessalonians 3:16.

"Keep yourselves in the love of God, looking for the mercy of our Lord Jesus Christ unto eternal life. And of some have compassion, making a difference."—Jude 21,22.

"God is our refuge and strength, a very present help in trouble."—Psalm 46:1.

**There is no grief like the grief
that does not speak.**

–Henry Wadsworth Longfellow

Growing in Christ

"Blessed is the man that trusteth in the LORD, and whose hope the LORD is. For he shall be as a tree planted by the waters, and that spreadeth out her roots by the river, and shall not see when heat cometh, but her leaf shall be green; and shall not be careful in the year of drought, neither shall cease from yielding fruit."—Jeremiah 17:7,8.

"And the child Samuel grew on, and was in favour both with the LORD, and also with men."—I Samuel 2:26.

"Being confident of this very thing, that he which hath begun a good work in you will perform it until the day of Jesus Christ."—Philippians 1:6.

"As ye have therefore received Christ Jesus the Lord, so walk ye in him: Rooted and built up in him, and stablished in the faith, as ye have been taught, abounding therein with thanksgiving."—Colossians 2:6,7.

Growing in Christ is advancing in one's Christian experience.
The only guide is God's Word.

"Not as though I had already attained, either were already perfect: but I follow after, if that I may apprehend that for which also I am apprehended of Christ Jesus. Brethren, I count not myself to have apprehended: but this one thing I do, forgetting those things which are behind, and reaching forth unto those things which are before, I press toward the mark for the prize of the high calling of God in Christ Jesus. Let us therefore, as many as be perfect, be thus minded: and if in any thing ye be otherwise minded, God shall reveal even this unto you. Nevertheless, whereto we have already attained, let us walk by the same rule, let us mind the same thing."—Philippians 3:12–16.

Never Quit!

"We are bound to thank God always for you, brethren, as it is meet, because that your faith groweth exceedingly, and the charity of every one of you all toward each other aboundeth." — II Thessalonians 1:3.

"Study to shew thyself approved unto God, a workman that needeth not to be ashamed, rightly dividing the word of truth." — II Timothy 2:15.

"My brethren, count it all joy when ye fall into divers temptations; Knowing this, that the trying of your faith worketh patience. But let patience have her perfect work, that ye may be perfect and entire, wanting nothing." — James 1:2–4.

"But grow in grace, and in the knowledge of our Lord and Saviour Jesus Christ. To him be glory both now and for ever. Amen." — II Peter 3:18.

"But ye, beloved, building up yourselves on your most holy faith, praying in the Holy Ghost." — Jude 20.

"For this cause we also, since the day we heard it, do not cease to pray for you, and to desire that ye might be filled with the knowledge of his will in all wisdom and spiritual understanding; That ye might walk worthy of the Lord unto all pleasing, being fruitful in every good work, and increasing in the knowledge of God; Strengthened with all might, according to his glorious power, unto all patience and long-suffering with joyfulness." — Colossians 1:9–11.

God has His best things for the few
Who dare to stand the test;
God has His second choice for those
Who will not have His best.

—A.B. Simpson

HAPPINESS

"Light is sown for the righteous, and gladness for the upright in heart."—Psalm 97:11.

"Delight thyself also in the LORD; and he shall give thee the desires of thine heart."—Psalm 37:4.

"The desire of the righteous is only good: but the expectation of the wicked is wrath."—Proverbs 11:23.

"...This day is holy unto our Lord: neither be ye sorry; for the joy of the LORD is your strength."—Nehemiah 8:10.

A wonderful source of happiness is a true faith
in Christ and his keeping power. Find
this source in His Word.

"Thou lovest righteousness, and hatest wickedness: therefore God, thy God, hath anointed thee with the oil of gladness above thy fellows."—Psalm 45:7.

"Serve the LORD with gladness: come before his presence with singing. Know ye that the LORD he is God: it is he that hath made us, and not we ourselves; we are his people, and the sheep of his pasture."—Psalm 100:2,3.

"Thy testimonies also are my delight and my counsellors."—Psalm 119:24.

"Happy is the man that findeth wisdom, and the man that getteth understanding....Her ways are ways of pleasantness, and all her paths are peace. She is a tree of life to them that lay hold upon her: and happy is every one that retaineth her."—Proverbs 3:13,17,18.

"Who redeemeth thy life from destruction; who crowneth thee with lovingkindness and tender mercies; Who satisfieth thy mouth with good things; so that thy youth is renewed like the eagle's."—Psalm 103:4,5.

"For thou shalt eat the labour of thine hands: happy shalt thou be, and it shall be well with thee."—Psalm 128:2.

"Whom having not seen, ye love; in whom, though now ye see him not, yet believing, ye rejoice with joy unspeakable and full of glory: Receiving the end of your faith, even the salvation of your souls."—I Peter 1:8,9.

"For I rejoiced greatly, when the brethren came and testified of the truth that is in thee, even as thou walkest in the truth. I have no greater joy than to hear that my children walk in truth."—III John 3,4.

"Now unto him that is able to keep you from falling, and to present you faultless before the presence of his glory with exceeding joy, To the only wise God our Saviour, be glory and majesty, dominion and power, both now and ever. Amen."—Jude 24,25.

Want a way to be miserable? Spend every hour of the day seeking for some way or some thing to make yourself happy. You find happines as you travel along helping others.

—Lindsay Terry

HARDSHIPS

"He shall call upon me, and I will answer him: I will be with him in trouble; I will deliver him, and honour him."—Psalm 91:15.

"Be not far from me; for trouble is near; for there is none to help."—Psalm 22:11.

"Nay, in all these things we are more than conquerors through him that loved us."—Romans 8:37.

"Take my yoke upon you, and learn of me; for I am meek and lowly in heart: and ye shall find rest unto your souls. For my yoke is easy, and my burden is light."—Matthew 11:29,30.

How would you know success and good times if you
were not acquainted with problems? Nothing
is superior except by comparison.

"Trust in the LORD with all thine heart; and lean not unto thine own understanding. In all thy ways acknowledge him, and he shall direct thy paths."—Proverbs 3:5,6.

"But we have this treasure in earthen vessels, that the excellency of the power may be of God, and not of us. We are troubled on every side, yet not distressed; we are perplexed, but not in despair."—II Corinthians 4:7,8.

"He healeth the broken in heart, and bindeth up their wounds."—Psalm 147:3.

"I can do all things through Christ which strengtheneth me."—Philippians 4:13.

71

"Let your conversation be without covetousness; and be content with such things as ye have: for he hath said, I will never leave thee, nor forsake thee. So that we may boldly say, The Lord is my helper, and I will not fear what man shall do unto me."—Hebrews 13:5,6.

"This poor man cried, and the LORD heard him, and saved him out of all his troubles."—Psalm 34:6.

"He giveth power to the faint; and to them that have no might he increaseth strength."—Isaiah 40:29.

"Many are the afflictions of the righteous: but the LORD delivereth him out of them all."—Psalm 34:19.

"Whoso keepeth his mouth and his tongue keepeth his soul from troubles."—Proverbs 21:2.

"I sought the LORD, and he heard me, and delivered me from all my fears."—Psalm 34:4.

To welcome a problem without resentment is to cut its size in half. We can spend our time aimlessly licking our wounds or aggressively licking our problems. Our Goliaths can be feared or fought, succumbed to or slain.

—William A. Ward

Most people spend more time and energy going around problems than in trying to solve them.

—Henry Ford

Heaven

"In my Father's house are many mansions: if it were not so, I would have told you. I go to prepare a place for you. And if I go and prepare a place for you, I will come again, and receive you unto myself; that where I am, there ye may be also."—John 14:2, 3.

"Beloved, now are we the sons of God, and it doth not yet appear what we shall be: but we know that, when he shall appear, we shall be like him; for we shall see him as he is."—I John 3:2.

"For Christ is not entered into the holy places made with hands, which are the figures of the true; but into heaven itself, now to appear in the presence of God for us."—Hebrews 9:24.

Heaven is our home with our Heavenly Father and
with all who have accepted Christ as Saviour.

"But now they desire a better country, that is, an heavenly: wherefore God is not ashamed to be called their God: for he hath prepared for them a city."—Hebrews 11:16.

"But ye are come unto mount Sion, and unto the city of the living God, the heavenly Jerusalem, and to an innumerable company of angels."—Hebrews 12:22.

"After this I beheld, and, lo, a great multitude, which no man could number, of all nations, and kindreds, and people, and tongues, stood before the throne, and before the Lamb, clothed with white robes, and palms in their hands."—Revelation 7:9.

"And I say unto you, That many shall come from the east and west, and shall sit down with Abraham, and Isaac, and Jacob, in the kingdom of heaven."—Matthew 8:11.

"And they sing the song of Moses the servant of God, and the song of the Lamb, saying, Great and marvellous are thy works, Lord God Almighty; just and true are thy ways, thou King of saints."—Revelation 15:3.

"And God shall wipe away all tears from their eyes; and there shall be no more death, neither sorrow, nor crying, neither shall there be any more pain: for the former things are passed away."—Revelation 21:4.

"For our conversation is in heaven; from whence also we look for the Saviour, the Lord Jesus Christ."—Philippians 3:20.

"And I saw no temple therein: for the Lord God Almighty and the Lamb are the temple of it. And the city had no need of the sun, neither of the moon, to shine in it: for the glory of God did lighten it, and the Lamb is the light thereof. And the nations of them which are saved shall walk in the light of it: and the kings of the earth do bring their glory and honour into it."—Revelation 21:22–24.

"And no man hath ascended up to heaven, but he that came down from heaven, even the Son of man which is in heaven."—John 3:13.

**This whole business of Someone else's providing
the way, Someone else's making provision,
so that forever and ever and ever I
can live, is an amazing thing!**
–Shelton L. Smith

HELL

"For if God spared not the angels that sinned, but cast them down to hell, and delivered them into chains of darkness, to be reserved unto judgment."—II Peter 2:4.

"The wicked shall be turned into hell, and all the nations that forget God."—Psalm 9:17.

"And I say also unto thee, That thou art Peter, and upon this rock I will build my church; and the gates of hell shall not prevail against it."—Matthew 16:18.

"And fear not them which kill the body, but are not able to kill the soul: but rather fear him which is able to destroy both soul and body in hell."—Matthew 10:28.

"And cast ye the unprofitable servant into outer darkness: there shall be weeping and gnashing of teeth."—Matthew 25:30.

A place of eternal separation from God, where those who have rejected Christ must go for all eternity.

"Stolen waters are sweet, and bread eaten in secret is pleasant. But he knoweth not that the dead are there; and that her guests are in the depths of hell."—Proverbs 9:17,18.

"Enter ye in at the strait gate: for wide is the gate, and broad is the way, that leadeth to destruction, and many there be which go in thereat."—Matthew 7:13.

"For God so loved the world, that he gave his only begotten Son, that whosoever believeth in him should not perish, but have everlasting life."—John 3:16.

"How shall we escape, if we neglect so great salvation; which at the first began to be spoken by the Lord, and was confirmed unto us by them that heard him."—Hebrews 2:3.

"And I say unto you my friends, Be not afraid of them that kill the body, and after that have no more that they can do. But I will forewarn you whom ye shall fear: Fear him, which after he hath killed hath power to cast into hell; yea, I say unto you, Fear him."—Luke 12:4,5.

"And the beast was taken, and with him the false prophet that wrought miracles before him, with which he deceived them that had received the mark of the beast, and them that worshipped his image. These both were cast alive into a lake of fire burning with brimstone."—Revelation 19:20.

"For the wages of sin is death; but the gift of God is eternal life through Jesus Christ our Lord."—Romans 6:23.

"I tell you, Nay: but, except ye repent, ye shall all likewise perish."—Luke 13:3.

Five seconds after death your soul will be in heaven or in hell.

—Lee Roberson

HOLY SPIRIT

"Turn you at my reproof: behold, I will pour out my Spirit unto you, I will make known my words unto you."—Proverbs 1:23.

"If ye then, being evil, know how to give good gifts unto your children: how much more shall your heavenly Father give the Holy Spirit to them that ask him?"—Luke 11:13.

"And I will pray the Father, and he shall give you another Comforter, that he may abide with you for ever; Even the Spirit of truth; whom the world cannot receive, because it seeth him not, neither knoweth him: but ye know him; for he dwelleth with you, and shall be in you."—John 14:16, 17.

"Likewise the Spirit also helpeth our infirmities: for we know not what we should pray for as we ought: but the Spirit itself maketh intercession for us with groanings which cannot be uttered. And he that searcheth the hearts knoweth what is the mind of the Spirit, because he maketh intercession for the saints according to the will of God."—Romans 8:26, 27.

The third Person of the Trinity, our Comforter and the One who speaks of Jesus.

"Howbeit when he, the Spirit of truth, is come, he will guide you into all truth: for he shall not speak of himself; but whatsoever he shall hear, that shall he speak: and he will shew you things to come."—John 16:13.

"And I will put my Spirit within you, and cause you to walk in my statutes, and ye shall keep my judgments, and do them."—Ezekiel 36:27.

"That the blessing of Abraham might come on the Gentiles through Jesus Christ; that we might receive the promise of the Spirit through faith."—Galatians 3:14.

"For the kingdom of God is not meat and drink; but righteousness, and peace, and joy in the Holy Ghost."—Romans 14:17.

"Now we have received, not the spirit of the world, but the spirit which is of God; that we might know the things that are freely given to us of God."—I Corinthians 2:12.

"For ye have not received the spirit of bondage again to fear; but ye have received the Spirit of adoption, whereby we cry, Abba, Father."—Romans 8:15.

"Cast me not away from thy presence; and take not thy holy spirit from me."—Psalm 51:11.

"And grieve not the holy Spirit of God, whereby ye are sealed unto the day of redemption."—Ephesians 4:30.

"He therefore that despiseth, despiseth not man, but God, who hath also given unto us his Holy Spirit."—I Thessalonians 4:8.

"In whom ye also trusted, after that ye heard the word of truth, the gospel of your salvation: in whom also after that ye believed, ye were sealed with that Holy Spirit of promise."—Ephesians 1:13.

The prime reason many believers do not have the fullness of the Holy Spirit is that they are not thirsty enough.

—Curtis Hutson

HOMOSEXUALITY

"And likewise also the men, leaving the natural use of the woman, burned in their lust one toward another; men with men working that which is unseemly, and receiving in themselves that recompence of their error which was meet. And even as they did not like to retain God in their knowledge, God gave them over to a reprobate mind, to do those things which are not convenient."—Romans 1:27,28.

"And they called unto Lot, and said unto him, Where are the men which came in to thee this night? bring them out unto us, that we may know them."—Genesis 19:5.

Sexual activity between those of the same sex.

"If a man also lie with mankind, as he lieth with a woman, both of them have committed an abomination: they shall surely be put to death; their blood shall be upon them."—Leviticus 20:13.

"Know ye not that the unrighteous shall not inherit the kingdom of God? Be not deceived: neither fornicators, nor idolaters, nor adulterers, nor effeminate, nor abusers of themselves with mankind, Nor thieves, nor covetous, nor drunkards, nor revilers, nor extortioners, shall inherit the kingdom of God."—I Corinthians 6:9,10.

"Thou shalt not lie with mankind, as with womankind: it is abomination. Neither shalt thou lie with any beast to defile thyself therewith: neither shall any woman stand before a beast to lie down thereto: it is confusion."—Leviticus 18:22,23.

"There shall be no whore of the daughters of Israel, nor a sodomite of the sons of Israel."—Deuteronomy 23:17.

"Now as they were making their hearts merry, behold, the men of the city, certain sons of Belial, beset the house round about, and beat at the door, and spake to the master of the house, the old man, saying, Bring forth the man that came into thine house, that we may know him. And the man, the master of the house, went out unto them, and said unto them, Nay, my brethren, nay, I pray you, do not so wickedly; seeing that this man is come into mine house, do not this folly. Behold, here is my daughter a maiden, and his concubine; them I will bring out now, and humble ye them, and do with them what seemeth good unto you: but unto this man do not so vile a thing."—Judges 19:22–24.

"And they have cast lots for my people; and have given a boy for an harlot, and sold a girl for wine, that they might drink."—Joel 3:3.

"For whoremongers, for them that defile themselves with mankind, for menstealers, for liars, for perjured persons, and if there be any other thing that is contrary to sound doctrine."—I Timothy 1:10.

"But every man is tempted, when he is drawn away of his own lust, and enticed. Then when lust hath conceived, it bringeth forth sin: and sin, when it is finished, bringeth forth death."—James 1:14,15.

"And there were also sodomites in the land: and they did according to all the abominations of the nations which the LORD cast out before the children of Israel."—I Kings 14:24.

No judgments will, of themselves, change the corrupt natures and purposes of wicked men.
—Matthew Henry

80

Humility

"O Lord, open thou my lips; and my mouth shall shew forth thy praise. For thou desirest not sacrifice; else would I give it: thou delightest not in burnt offering. The sacrifices of God are a broken spirit: a broken and a contrite heart, O God, thou wilt not despise."—Psalm 51:15–17.

"For promotion cometh neither from the east, nor from the west, nor from the south. But God is the judge: he putteth down one, and setteth up another."—Psalm 75:6,7.

"I am not worthy of the least of all the mercies, and of all the truth, which thou hast shewed unto thy servant; for with my staff I passed over this Jordan; and now I am become two bands."—Genesis 32:10.

"Let this mind be in you, which was also in Christ Jesus: Who, being in the form of God, thought it not robbery to be equal with God: But made himself of no reputation, and took upon him the form of a servant, and was made in the likeness of men: And being found in fashion as a man, he humbled himself, and became obedient unto death, even the death of the cross."—Philippians 2:5–8.

A humble person will think first of the needs of others and
will not be at all impressed with his or her own
accomplishments or things possessed.

"If my people, which are called by my name, shall humble themselves, and pray, and seek my face, and turn from their wicked ways; then will I hear from heaven, and will forgive their sin, and will heal their land."—II Chronicles 7:14.

"Surely he scorneth the scorners: but he giveth grace unto the lowly."—Proverbs 3:34.

"The fear of the LORD is the instruction of wisdom; and before honour is humility."—Proverbs 15:33.

"By humility and the fear of the LORD are riches, and honour, and life."—Proverbs 22:4.

"Whosoever therefore shall humble himself as this little child, the same is greatest in the kingdom of heaven."—Matthew 18:4.

"But he giveth more grace. Wherefore he saith, God resisteth the proud, but giveth grace unto the humble."—James 4:6.

"Humble yourselves therefore under the mighty hand of God, that he may exalt you in due time."—I Peter 5:6.

"But by the grace of God I am what I am: and his grace which was bestowed upon me was not in vain; but I laboured more abundantly than they all: yet not I, but the grace of God which was with me."—I Corinthians 15:10.

True humility is not an abject, groveling, self-despising spirit; it is but a right estimate of ourselves as God sees us.

—Tryon Edwards

HYPOCRISY

"And why beholdest thou the mote that is in thy brother's eye, but perceivest not the beam that is in thine own eye? Either how canst thou say to thy brother, Brother, let me pull out the mote that is in thine eye, when thou thyself beholdest not the beam that is in thine own eye? Thou hypocrite, cast out first the beam out of thine own eye, and then shalt thou see clearly to pull out the mote that is in thy brother's eye." —Luke 6:41, 42.

"They profess that they know God; but in works they deny him, being abominable, and disobedient, and unto every good work reprobate." —Titus 1:16.

"Woe unto you, scribes and Pharisees, hypocrites! for ye are like unto whited sepulchres, which indeed appear beautiful outward, but are within full of dead men's bones, and of all uncleanness." —Matthew 23:27.

An attitude of pretentiousness.
Acting as if one holds to virtues or feelings
that he or she does not possess.

"Shall we give, or shall we not give? But he, knowing their hypocrisy, said unto them, Why tempt ye me? bring me a penny, that I may see it." —Mark 12:15.

"But the wisdom that is from above is first pure, then peaceable, gentle, and easy to be intreated, full of mercy and good fruits, without partiality, and without hypocrisy." — James 3:17.

"He also shall be my salvation: for an hypocrite shall not come before him." —Job 13:16.

"Therefore thou art inexcusable, O man, whosoever thou art that judgest: for wherein thou judgest another, thou condemnest thyself; for thou that judgest doest the same things."—Romans 2:1.

"Ye hypocrites, ye can discern the face of the sky and of the earth; but how is it that ye do not discern this time?"—Luke 12:56.

"Then said he to the multitude that came forth to be baptized of him, O generation of vipers, who hath warned you to flee from the wrath to come? Bring forth therefore fruits worthy of repentance, and begin not to say within yourselves, We have Abraham to our father: for I say unto you, That God is able of these stones to raise up children unto Abraham."—Luke 3:7,8.

"Now the Spirit speaketh expressly, that in the latter times some shall depart from the faith, giving heed to seducing spirits, and doctrines of devils; Speaking lies in hypocrisy; having their conscience seared with a hot iron."—I Timothy 4:1,2.

"Wherefore laying aside all malice, and all guile, and hypocrisies, and envies, and all evil speakings."—I Peter 2:1.

Despicable and wrong indeed is the person who professes what he does not possess.
—Unknown

It is an awful hypocrisy that declares with the lips what it denies with the life.
—Vance Havner

ILLICIT DRUG ABUSE

"For the time past of our life may suffice us to have wrought the will of the Gentiles, when we walked in lasciviousness, lusts, excess of wine, revellings, banquetings, and abominable idolatries."—I Peter 4:3.

"But every man is tempted, when he is drawn away of his own lust, and enticed. Then when lust hath conceived, it bringeth forth sin: and sin, when it is finished, bringeth forth death."—James 1:14, 15.

"There hath no temptation taken you but such as is common to man: but God is faithful, who will not suffer you to be tempted above that ye are able; but will with the temptation also make a way to escape, that ye may be able to bear it."—I Corinthians 10:13.

"For God hath not given us the spirit of fear; but of power, and of love, and of a sound mind."—II Timothy 1:7.

Using mind-altering substances.

"And ye shall know the truth, and the truth shall make you free....If the Son therefore shall make you free, ye shall be free indeed."—John 8:32, 36.

"Why art thou cast down, O my soul? and why art thou disquieted within me? hope thou in God: for I shall yet praise him, who is the health of my countenance, and my God."—Psalm 42:11.

"I sought the LORD, and he heard me, and delivered me from all my fears. They looked unto him, and were lightened: and their faces were not ashamed."—Psalm 34:4, 5.

"Casting all your care upon him; for he careth for you."—
I Peter 5:7.

"Trust in the LORD with all thine heart; and lean not unto thine own understanding. In all thy ways acknowledge him, and he shall direct thy paths."—Proverbs 3:5, 6.

"Come unto me, all ye that labour and are heavy laden, and I will give you rest."—Matthew 11:28.

"Trust ye in the LORD for ever: for in the LORD JEHOVAH is everlasting strength: For he bringeth down them that dwell on high; the lofty city, he layeth it low; he layeth it low, even to the ground; he bringeth it even to the dust."—Isaiah 26:4, 5.

"Therefore, brethren, we are debtors, not to the flesh, to live after the flesh. For if ye live after the flesh, ye shall die: but if ye through the Spirit do mortify the deeds of the body, ye shall live."—Romans 8:12, 13.

"And they that are Christ's have crucified the flesh with the affections and lusts."—Galatians 5:24.

There is no doubt about it. Almost every drug addict I've talked to said he started with marijuana.

**—Chief John Enright
Federal Bureau of
Narcotics and Dangerous
Drugs**

ILLNESS

"Is any sick among you? let him call for the elders of the church; and let them pray over him, anointing him with oil in the name of the Lord: And the prayer of faith shall save the sick, and the Lord shall raise him up; and if he have committed sins, they shall be forgiven him. Confess your faults one to another, and pray one for another, that ye may be healed. The effectual fervent prayer of a righteous man availeth much."—James 5:14–16.

"For it became him, for whom are all things, and by whom are all things, in bringing many sons unto glory, to make the captain of their salvation perfect through sufferings."—Hebrews 2:10.

"The LORD will strengthen him upon the bed of languishing: thou wilt make all his bed in his sickness."—Psalm 41:3.

"For I will restore health unto thee, and I will heal thee of thy wounds, saith the LORD; because they called thee an outcast, saying, This is Zion, whom no man seeketh after."—Jeremiah 30:17.

Illness is a time when we trust God for our healing. God does not always direct that one be ill; sometimes he simply allows it.

"And ye shall serve the LORD your God, and he shall bless thy bread, and thy water; and I will take sickness away from the midst of thee."—Exodus 23:25.

"And when he was come into the house, the blind men came to him: and Jesus saith unto them, Believe ye that I am able to do this? They said unto him, Yea, Lord."—Matthew 9:28.

"Bless the LORD, O my soul, and forget not all his benefits: Who forgiveth all thine iniquities; who healeth all thy diseases."—Psalm 103:2,3.

"And not only so, but we glory in tribulations also: knowing that tribulation worketh patience."—Romans 5:3.

"Forasmuch then as Christ hath suffered for us in the flesh, arm yourselves likewise with the same mind: for he that hath suffered in the flesh hath ceased from sin; That he no longer should live the rest of his time in the flesh to the lusts of men, but to the will of God."—I Peter 4:1,2.

"Wherein ye greatly rejoice, though now for a season, if need be, ye are in heaviness through manifold temptations: That the trial of your faith, being much more precious than of gold that perisheth, though it be tried with fire, might be found unto praise and honour and glory at the appearing of Jesus Christ."—I Peter 1:6,7.

"That it might be fulfilled which was spoken by Esaias the prophet, saying, Himself took our infirmities, and bare our sicknesses."—Matthew 8:17.

"And Jesus went about all Galilee, teaching in their synagogues, and preaching the gospel of the kingdom, and healing all manner of sickness and all manner of disease among the people."—Matthew 4:23.

What we count the ills of life are often blessings
in disguise resulting in good to us in the end.
Though for the present not joyous but
grievous, yet if received in a right spirit,
they work out fruits of righteousness
for us at last.

–Matthew Henry

INTEGRITY

"My brethren, count it all joy when ye fall into divers temptations; Knowing this, that the trying of your faith worketh patience. But let patience have her perfect work, that ye may be perfect and entire, wanting nothing."—James 1:2–4.

"A false balance is abomination to the LORD: but a just weight is his delight."—Proverbs 11:1.

"My righteousness I hold fast, and will not let it go: my heart shall not reproach me so long as I live."—Job 27:6.

"Even a child is known by his doings, whether his work be pure, and whether it be right."—Proverbs 20:11.

Integrity encompasses several character traits, such as
fairness, honesty, faithfulness and thrift. It is
a godly manner in which to live.

"And herein do I exercise myself, to have always a conscience void of offence toward God, and toward men."—Acts 24:16.

"As the fining pot for silver, and the furnace for gold; so is a man to his praise."—Proverbs 27:21.

"The just man walketh in his integrity: his children are blessed after him."—Proverbs 20:7.

"He that walketh righteously, and speaketh uprightly; he that despiseth the gain of oppressions, that shaketh his hands from holding of bribes, that stoppeth his ears from hearing of blood, and shutteth his eyes from seeing evil."—Isaiah 33:15.

"Thus saith the LORD; *Execute ye judgment and righteousness, and deliver the spoiled out of the hand of the oppressor: and do no wrong, do no violence to the stranger, the fatherless, nor the widow, neither shed innocent blood in this place."*—Jeremiah 22:3.

"Therefore all things whatsoever ye would that men should do to you, do ye even so to them: for this is the law and the prophets."—Matthew 7:12.

"But your iniquities have separated between you and your God, and your sins have hid his face from you, that he will not hear. For your hands are defiled with blood, and your fingers with iniquity; your lips have spoken lies, your tongue hath muttered perverseness."—Isaiah 59:2, 3.

"Thou shalt destroy them that speak leasing: the LORD *will abhor the bloody and deceitful man."*—Psalm 5:6.

"A false witness shall not be unpunished, and he that speaketh lies shall not escape."—Proverbs 19:5.

"Blessed is the man unto whom the LORD *imputeth not iniquity, and in whose spirit there is no guile."*—Psalm 32:2.

**A man of integrity will never listen
to any pleas against conscience.**
–Unknown

JEALOUSY

"A sound heart is the life of the flesh: but envy the rottenness of the bones."—Proverbs 14:30.

"Envy thou not the oppressor, and choose none of his ways."—Proverbs 3:31.

"Wrath is cruel, and anger is outrageous; but who is able to stand before envy?"—Proverbs 27:4.

"For where envying and strife is, there is confusion and every evil work."—James 3:16.

"Let your conversation be without covetousness; and be content with such things as ye have: for he hath said, I will never leave thee, nor forsake thee."—Hebrews 13:5.

The green-eyed monster who causes men and women to hold terrible attitudes toward others' fortunes.
A destroyer of homes.

"Let not thine heart envy sinners: but be thou in the fear of the LORD all the day long."—Proverbs 23:17.

"And he said unto them, Take heed, and beware of covetousness: for a man's life consisteth not in the abundance of the things which he possesseth."—Luke 12:15.

"For wrath killeth the foolish man, and envy slayeth the silly one."—Job 5:2.

"Let us walk honestly, as in the day; not in rioting and drunkenness, not in chambering and wantonness, not in strife and envying."—Romans 13:13.

"*Charity suffereth long, and is kind; charity envieth not; charity vaunteth not itself, is not puffed up.*"—I Corinthians 13:4.

"*For ye are yet carnal: for whereas there is among you envying, and strife, and divisions, are ye not carnal, and walk as men?*"—I Corinthians 3:3.

"*But if ye have bitter envying and strife in your hearts, glory not, and lie not against the truth.*"—James 3:14.

"*Envyings, murders, drunkenness, revellings, and such like: of the which I tell you before, as I have also told you in time past, that they which do such things shall not inherit the kingdom of God.*"—Galatians 5:21.

Nothing is more destructive than jealousy. The wise Solomon said that jealousy is as cruel as the grave. It burns with a vehement heat.

—Raymond Barber

KINDNESS

"And be ye kind one to another, tenderhearted, forgiving one another, even as God for Christ's sake hath forgiven you." —Ephesians 4:32.

"Then shall the King say unto them on his right hand, Come, ye blessed of my Father, inherit the kingdom prepared for you from the foundation of the world: For I was an hungred, and ye gave me meat: I was thirsty, and ye gave me drink: I was a stranger, and ye took me in: Naked, and ye clothed me: I was sick, and ye visited me: I was in prison, and ye came unto me." —Matthew 25:34–36.

Kindness is an important attitude for Christians.
Only with this characteristic will we be
aware of the needs of others.

"And if ye lend to them of whom ye hope to receive, what thank have ye? for sinners also lend to sinners, to receive as much again. But love ye your enemies, and do good, and lend, hoping for nothing again; and your reward shall be great, and ye shall be the children of the Highest: for he is kind unto the unthankful and to the evil." —Luke 6:34, 35.

"And beside this, giving all diligence, add to your faith virtue; and to virtue knowledge; And to knowledge temperance; and to temperance patience; and to patience godliness; And to godliness brotherly kindness; and to brotherly kindness charity." —II Peter 1:5–7.

"And he said, Blessed be thou of the LORD, my daughter: for thou hast shewed more kindness in the latter end than at the beginning, inasmuch as thou followedst not young men, whether poor or rich." —Ruth 3:10.

93

"Put on therefore, as the elect of God, holy and beloved, bowels of mercies, kindness, humbleness of mind, meekness, longsuffering."—Colossians 3:12.

"Because thy lovingkindness is better than life, my lips shall praise thee."—Psalm 63:3.

"For his merciful kindness is great toward us: and the truth of the LORD *endureth for ever. Praise ye the* LORD.*"*—Psalm 117:2.

"Let, I pray thee, thy merciful kindness be for my comfort, according to thy word unto thy servant."—Psalm 119:76.

"She openeth her mouth with wisdom; and in her tongue is the law of kindness."—Proverbs 31:26.

"And Naomi said unto her two daughters in law, Go, return each to her mother's house: the LORD *deal kindly with you, as ye have dealt with the dead, and with me."*—Ruth 1:8.

"Be kindly affectioned one to another with brotherly love; in honour preferring one another."—Romans 12:10.

"In a little wrath I hid my face from thee for a moment; but with everlasting kindness will I have mercy on thee, saith the LORD *thy Redeemer."*—Isaiah 54:8.

"Go and cry in the ears of Jerusalem, saying, Thus saith the LORD; *I remember thee, the kindness of thy youth, the love of thine espousals, when thou wentest after me in the wilderness, in a land that was not sown."*—Jeremiah 2:2.

**Kindness in ourselves is the honey that blunts
the sting of unkindness in another.**
—Landor

LAZINESS

"Be kindly affectioned one to another with brotherly love; in honour preferring one another; Not slothful in business; fervent in spirit; serving the Lord."—Romans 12:10,11.

"As vinegar to the teeth, and as smoke to the eyes, so is the sluggard to them that send him."—Proverbs 10:26.

"The sluggard will not plow by reason of the cold; therefore shall he beg in harvest, and have nothing."—Proverbs 20:4.

"Go to the ant, thou sluggard; consider her ways, and be wise."—Proverbs 6:6.

"For God is not unrighteous to forget your work and labour of love, which ye have shewed toward his name, in that ye have ministered to the saints, and do minister. And we desire that every one of you do shew the same diligence to the full assurance of hope unto the end: That ye be not slothful, but followers of them who through faith and patience inherit the promises."—Hebrews 6:10–12.

Often an able-bodied person tries to convince himself
that he is justified in not performing a certain task
that needs to be done, solely because he doesn't
want to do it—a miserable soul, indeed.

"The soul of the sluggard desireth, and hath nothing: but the soul of the diligent shall be made fat."—Proverbs 13:4.

"The sluggard is wiser in his own conceit than seven men that can render a reason."—Proverbs 26:16.

"Yet a little sleep, a little slumber, a little folding of the hands to sleep: So shall thy poverty come as one that travelleth, and thy want as an armed man."—Proverbs 6:10, 11.

"Love not sleep, lest thou come to poverty; open thine eyes, and thou shalt be satisfied with bread."—Proverbs 20:13.

"He also that is slothful in his work is brother to him that is a great waster."—Proverbs 18:9.

Laziness grows on people; it begins in
cobwebs and ends in iron chains.

—Thomas Buxton

Excess is not the only thing that breaks up both
health and enjoyment; many are brought into
a very ill and languishing habit of body by
mere sloth, which is both a great sin
and the cause of many more.

—Robert South

LEADERSHIP

"That ye be not slothful, but followers of them who through faith and patience inherit the promises."—Hebrews 6:12.

"Remember them which have the rule over you, who have spoken unto you the word of God: whose faith follow, considering the end of their conversation."—Hebrews 13:7.

"Let no man despise thy youth; but be thou an example of the believers, in word, in conversation, in charity, in spirit, in faith, in purity."—I Timothy 4:12.

"Those things, which ye have both learned, and received, and heard, and seen in me, do: and the God of peace shall be with you."—Philippians 4:9.

Leadership is a gift from God. It can be honed and improved in some people, but it cannot be taught. God is the One who places it within the breast of certain individuals.

"And when James, Cephas, and John, who seemed to be pillars, perceived the grace that was given unto me, they gave to me and Barnabas the right hands of fellowship; that we should go unto the heathen, and they unto the circumcision."—Galatians 2:9.

"For even hereunto were ye called: because Christ also suffered for us, leaving us an example, that ye should follow his steps."—I Peter 2:21.

"And ye became followers of us, and of the Lord, having received the word in much affliction, with joy of the Holy Ghost."—I Thessalonians 1:6.

"Thou leddest thy people like a flock by the hand of Moses and Aaron."—Psalm 77:20.

"And who is he that will harm you, if ye be followers of that which is good?"—I Peter 3:13.

"Let him that is taught in the word communicate unto him that teacheth in all good things."—Galatians 6:6.

A leader has been defined as one who knows the way, goes the way and shows the way.

–Unknown

A man who follows a crowd will never be followed by a crowd.

–John Maxwell

LIFE'S GOALS

"And let us not be weary in well doing: for in due season we shall reap, if we faint not."—Galatians 6:9.

"I therefore so run, not as uncertainly; so fight I, not as one that beateth the air."—I Corinthians 9:26.

"See then that ye walk circumspectly, not as fools, but as wise, Redeeming the time, because the days are evil."—Ephesians 5:15, 16.

"Let thine eyes look right on, and let thine eyelids look straight before thee. Ponder the path of thy feet, and let all thy ways be established. Turn not to the right hand nor to the left: remove thy foot from evil."—Proverbs 4:25–27.

"Wherefore we labour, that, whether present or absent, we may be accepted of him."—II Corinthians 5:9.

Although both are important and can lead to
success in life, short-term goals are more
important than long-term ambitions.

"My son, let not them depart from thine eyes: keep sound wisdom and discretion: So shall they be life unto thy soul, and grace to thy neck."—Proverbs 3:21, 22.

"Now the end of the commandment is charity out of a pure heart, and of a good conscience, and of faith unfeigned."—I Timothy 1:5.

"The thoughts of the diligent tend only to plenteousness; but of every one that is hasty only to want."—Proverbs 21:5.

NEVER QUIT!

"He that gathereth in summer is a wise son: but he that sleepeth in harvest is a son that causeth shame."—Proverbs 10:5.

"Delight thyself also in the LORD; and he shall give thee the desires of thine heart. Commit thy way unto the LORD; trust also in him; and he shall bring it to pass."—Psalm 37:4,5.

"The preparations of the heart in man, and the answer of the tongue, is from the LORD."—Proverbs 16:1.

"Walk in wisdom toward them that are without, redeeming the time."—Colossians 4:5.

"I press toward the mark for the prize of the high calling of God in Christ Jesus."—Philippians 3:14.

Your goals must be strong enough to offset any defeat or humiliation.

—W. Jack Hudson

MEEKNESS

"Now the man Moses was very meek, above all the men which were upon the face of the earth."—Numbers 12:3.

"The meek shall eat and be satisfied: they shall praise the LORD that seek him: your heart shall live for ever."—Psalm 22:26.

"Blessed are the meek: for they shall inherit the earth."—Matthew 5:5.

"And be ye kind one to another, tenderhearted, forgiving one another, even as God for Christ's sake hath forgiven you."—Ephesians 4:32.

"For the LORD taketh pleasure in his people: he will beautify the meek with salvation."—Psalm 149:4.

"Now I Paul myself beseech you by the meekness and gentleness of Christ, who in presence am base among you, but being absent am bold toward you."—II Corinthians 10:1.

Good examples of meekness are Moses and David in the
Old Testament. They were not impressed by their
strength or ability, but knew how to control it.

"Judge not, and ye shall not be judged: condemn not, and ye shall not be condemned: forgive, and ye shall be forgiven."—Luke 6:37.

"Take my yoke upon you, and learn of me; for I am meek and lowly in heart: and ye shall find rest unto your souls."—Matthew 11:29.

"He that is slow to anger is better than the mighty; and he that ruleth his spirit than he that taketh a city."—Proverbs 16:32.

"The discretion of a man deferreth his anger; and it is his glory to pass over a transgression."—Proverbs 19:11.

"A soft answer turneth away wrath: but grievous words stir up anger."—Proverbs 15:1.

"Mercy and truth are met together; righteousness and peace have kissed each other. Truth shall spring out of the earth; and righteousness shall look down from heaven."—Psalm 85:10,11.

"Great peace have they which love thy law: and nothing shall offend them."—Psalm 119:165.

"But the meek shall inherit the earth; and shall delight themselves in the abundance of peace."—Psalm 37:11.

Meekness cannot well be counterfeited. It is not insensibility or unmanliness or servility; it does not cringe or whine. It is benevolence imitating Christ in patience, forbearance and quietness. It feels keenly but not malignantly; it abounds in goodwill and bears all things.

—W. S. Plummer

MISSIONS

"Go ye therefore, and teach all nations, baptizing them in the name of the Father, and of the Son, and of the Holy Ghost: Teaching them to observe all things whatsoever I have commanded you: and, lo, I am with you alway, even unto the end of the world. Amen."—Matthew 28:19,20.

"Say not ye, There are yet four months, and then cometh harvest? behold, I say unto you, Lift up your eyes, and look on the fields; for they are white already to harvest."—John 4:35.

Getting the Gospel of Christ to people who have never trusted in the Savior—usually in other countries where there are few opportunities to hear.

"For I am not ashamed of the gospel of Christ: for it is the power of God unto salvation to every one that believeth; to the Jew first, and also to the Greek."—Romans 1:16.

"Pray ye therefore the Lord of the harvest, that he will send forth labourers into his harvest."—Matthew 9:38.

"Neither is there salvation in any other: for there is none other name under heaven given among men, whereby we must be saved."—Acts 4:12.

"To him give all the prophets witness, that through his name whosoever believeth in him shall receive remission of sins."—Acts 10:43.

"By whom we have received grace and apostleship, for obedience to the faith among all nations, for his name."—Romans 1:5.

103

"But to Israel he saith, All day long I have stretched forth my hands unto a disobedient and gainsaying people."—Romans 10:21.

"For the wrath of God is revealed from heaven against all ungodliness and unrighteousness of men, who hold the truth in unrighteousness; Because that which may be known of God is manifest in them; for God hath shewed it unto them. For the invisible things of him from the creation of the world are clearly seen, being understood by the things that are made, even his eternal power and Godhead; so that they are without excuse: Because that, when they knew God, they glorified him not as God, neither were thankful; but became vain in their imaginations, and their foolish heart was darkened."—Romans 1:18–21.

"For by him were all things created, that are in heaven, and that are in earth, visible and invisible, whether they be thrones, or dominions, or principalities, or powers: all things were created by him, and for him: And he is before all things, and by him all things consist."—Colossians 1:16,17.

"Jesus saith unto him, I am the way, the truth, and the life: no man cometh unto the Father, but by me."—John 14:6.

"For this is good and acceptable in the sight of God our Saviour; Who will have all men to be saved, and to come unto the knowledge of the truth."—I Timothy 2:3,4.

I have but one candle of life to burn, and I would rather burn it in a land filled with darkness than a land flooded with lights.
—John Keith Falconer

OBEYING GOD

"By this we know that we love the children of God, when we love God, and keep his commandments. For this is the love of God, that we keep his commandments: and his commandments are not grievous."—I John 5:2–3.

"Blessed are they that keep his testimonies, and that seek him with the whole heart."—Psalm 119:2.

"Children, obey your parents in all things: for this is well pleasing unto the Lord."—Colossians 3:20.

"Obey them that have the rule over you, and submit yourselves: for they watch for your souls, as they that must give account, that they may do it with joy, and not with grief: for that is unprofitable for you."—Hebrews 13:17.

"Children, obey your parents in the Lord: for this is right."—Ephesians 6:1.

Obedience starts when small children learn to be obedient to
their parents and adults placed in charge. This obedience,
for Christians, can result in wonderful peace and
happiness in their lives.

"For not the hearers of the law are just before God, but the doers of the law shall be justified."—Romans 2:13.

"Let every soul be subject unto the higher powers. For there is no power but of God: the powers that be are ordained of God."—Romans 13:1.

"Then Peter and the other apostles answered and said, We ought to obey God rather than men."—Acts 5:29.

"Wherefore gird up the loins of your mind, be sober, and hope to the end for the grace that is to be brought unto you at the revelation of Jesus Christ; As obedient children, not fashioning yourselves according to the former lusts in your ignorance."—I Peter 1:13, 14.

"By faith Abraham, when he was called to go out into a place which he should after receive for an inheritance, obeyed; and he went out, not knowing whither he went."— Hebrews 11:8.

"And we are his witnesses of these things; and so is also the Holy Ghost, whom God hath given to them that obey him."—Acts 5:32.

"Ye shall observe to do therefore as the LORD your God hath commanded you: ye shall not turn aside to the right hand or to the left."—Deuteronomy 5:32.

"But Peter and John answered and said unto them, Whether it be right in the sight of God to hearken unto you more than unto God, judge ye. For we cannot but speak the things which we have seen and heard."—Acts 4:19, 20.

"For to this end also did I write, that I might know the proof of you, whether ye be obedient in all things."— II Corinthians 2:9.

The golden rule for understanding spiritually is not intellect but obedience. If a man wants... insight into what Jesus Christ teaches, he can only get it by obedience.

—Oswald Chambers

OTHERS

"And thou shalt love the Lord thy God with all thy heart, and with all thy soul, and with all thy mind, and with all thy strength: this is the first commandment. And the second is like, namely this, Thou shalt love thy neighbour as thyself. There is none other commandment greater than these."—Mark 12:30,31.

"A friend loveth at all times, and a brother is born for adversity."—Proverbs 17:17.

"This is my commandment, That ye love one another, as I have loved you."—John 15:12.

"We then that are strong ought to bear the infirmities of the weak, and not to please ourselves."—Romans 15:1.

"But I say unto you which hear, Love your enemies, do good to them which hate you."—Luke 6:27.

Jesus' second-favorite commandment was wrapped around this subject: loving your neighbor as yourself.

"Therefore all things whatsoever ye would that men should do to you, do ye even so to them: for this is the law and the prophets."—Matthew 7:12.

"He that hath pity upon the poor lendeth unto the LORD; and that which he hath given will he pay him again."—Proverbs 19:17.

"Bear ye one another's burdens, and so fulfil the law of Christ."—Galatians 6:2.

NEVER QUIT!

"But a certain Samaritan, as he journeyed, came where he was: and when he saw him, he had compassion on him, And went to him, and bound up his wounds, pouring in oil and wine, and set him on his own beast, and brought him to an inn, and took care of him."—Luke 10:33, 34.

"He that hath a bountiful eye shall be blessed; for he giveth of his bread to the poor."—Proverbs 22:9.

"And if thou draw out thy soul to the hungry, and satisfy the afflicted soul; then shall thy light rise in obscurity, and thy darkness be as the noonday."—Isaiah 58:10.

"Honour all men. Love the brotherhood. Fear God. Honour the king."—I Peter 2:17.

"A man that hath friends must shew himself friendly: and there is a friend that sticketh closer than a brother."—Proverbs 18:24.

> Others, Lord, yes, others—
> Let this my motto be.
> Help me to live for others,
> That I might live like Thee.

> And when my work on earth is done
> And my new work in heaven begun,
> May I forget the crown I've won
> While thinking still of others.
>
> —C. D. Meigs

PATIENCE

"Behold, we count them happy which endure. Ye have heard of the patience of Job, and have seen the end of the Lord; that the Lord is very pitiful, and of tender mercy."— James 5:1.

"I wait for the LORD, my soul doth wait, and in his word do I hope. My soul waiteth for the Lord more than they that watch for the morning: I say, more than they that watch for the morning."—Psalm 130:5,6.

"I waited patiently for the LORD; and he inclined unto me, and heard my cry."—Psalm 40:1.

"And not only so, but we glory in tribulations also: knowing that tribulation worketh patience; And patience, experience; and experience, hope."—Romans 5:3,4.

"Stand in awe, and sin not: commune with your own heart upon your bed, and be still. Selah."—Psalm 4:4.

"Wait on the LORD, and keep his way, and he shall exalt thee to inherit the land: when the wicked are cut off, thou shalt see it."—Psalm 37:34.

In the lives of most successful men, we find an unalterable and massive amount of patience. Job is noted for it, we pray to possess it, and God is the Master of it. The word comes from a Greek word which means to "stay under," waiting until the right time to take action or to come forth.

"And it shall be said in that day, Lo, this is our God; we have waited for him, and he will save us: this is the LORD; we have waited for him, we will be glad and rejoice in his salvation."—Isaiah 25:9.

109

"*Because to every purpose there is time and judgment, therefore the misery of man is great upon him.*"— Ecclesiastes 8:6.

"*The* Lord *is longsuffering, and of great mercy, forgiving iniquity and transgression, and by no means clearing the guilty, visiting the iniquity of the fathers upon the children unto the third and fourth generation.*"—Numbers 14:18.

"*That ye be not slothful, but followers of them who through faith and patience inherit the promises.*"—Hebrews 6:12.

"*My brethren, count it all joy when ye fall into divers temptations; Knowing this, that the trying of your faith worketh patience. But let patience have her perfect work, that ye may be perfect and entire, wanting nothing.*"—James 1:2–4.

"*Strengthened with all might, according to his glorious power, unto all patience and longsuffering with joyfulness.*"— Colossians 1:11.

"*Rejoicing in hope; patient in tribulation; continuing instant in prayer.*"—Romans 12:12.

As a Christian grows more patient, he will begin to gain necessary experience in his relationship with God. Experiences in which God intervenes and shows Himself to be God are the results of patience.

–David C. Gibbs, Jr.

PEER PRESSURE

"And be not conformed to this world: but be ye trans-formed by the renewing of your mind, that ye may prove what is that good, and acceptable, and perfect, will of God."—Romans 12:2.

"Wherefore come out from among them, and be ye sepa-rate, saith the Lord, and touch not the unclean thing; and I will receive you, And will be a Father unto you, and ye shall be my sons and daughters, saith the Lord Almighty."— II Corinthians 6:17,18.

"But sanctify the Lord God in your hearts: and be ready always to give an answer to every man that asketh you a reason of the hope that is in you with meekness and fear: Having a good conscience; that, whereas they speak evil of you, as of evildoers, they may be ashamed that falsely accuse your good conversation in Christ."—I Peter 3:15,16.

"That ye would walk worthy of God, who hath called you unto his kingdom and glory."—I Thessalonians 2:12.

The strong pull of the friends around you to
go in their direction, either for good or for
evil. An intense desire to be accepted.

"Abstain from all appearance of evil."—I Thessalonians 5:22.

"As obedient children, not fashioning yourselves accord-ing to the former lusts in your ignorance: But as he which hath called you is holy, so be ye holy in all manner of con-versation; Because it is written, Be ye holy; for I am holy."— I Peter 1:14–16.

111

"For God hath not called us unto uncleanness, but unto holiness."—I Thessalonians 4:7.

"Depart from evil, and do good; seek peace, and pursue it."—Psalm 34:14.

"And now, little children, abide in him; that, when he shall appear, we may have confidence, and not be ashamed before him at his coming."—I John 2:28.

"And ye know that he was manifested to take away our sins; and in him is no sin. Whosoever abideth in him sinneth not: whosoever sinneth hath not seen him, neither known him."—I John 3:5, 6.

"I will meditate in thy precepts, and have respect unto thy ways. I will delight myself in thy statutes: I will not forget thy word."—Psalm 119:15, 16.

"But put ye on the Lord Jesus Christ, and make not provision for the flesh, to fulfil the lusts thereof."—Romans 13:14.

"Let not mercy and truth forsake thee: bind them about thy neck; write them upon the table of thine heart: So shalt thou find favour and good understanding in the sight of God and man."—Proverbs 3:3, 4.

"A good name is rather to be chosen than great riches, and loving favour rather than silver and gold."—Proverbs 22:1.

**One matron to another in a swank restaurant:
"We're trying to enlarge our circle of friends
to include people we like."**

POVERTY

"For ye know the grace of our Lord Jesus Christ, that, though he was rich, yet for your sakes he became poor, that ye through his poverty might be rich."—II Corinthians 8:9.

"For the drunkard and the glutton shall come to poverty: and drowsiness shall clothe a man with rags."—Proverbs 23:21.

"Take thou no usury of him, or increase: but fear thy God; that thy brother may live with thee."—Leviticus 25:36.

"How much less to him that accepteth not the persons of princes, nor regardeth the rich more than the poor? for they all are the work of his hands."—Job 34:19.

"For the needy shall not alway be forgotten: the expectation of the poor shall not perish for ever."—Psalm 9:18.

"I was a father to the poor: and the cause which I knew not I searched out."—Job 29:16.

Jesus said that they would always be with us, yet we have
a godly obligation to do that which is in our power to
ease the plight of genuinely poor people. While
here on the earth, Jesus was poor.

"For the LORD heareth the poor, and despiseth not his prisoners."—Psalm 69:33.

"Lest I be full, and deny thee, and say, Who is the LORD? or lest I be poor, and steal, and take the name of my God in vain."—Proverbs 30:9.

"He will regard the prayer of the destitute, and not despise their prayer."—Psalm 102:17.

"For he shall deliver the needy when he crieth; the poor also, and him that hath no helper."—Psalm 72:12.

"Hearken, my beloved brethren, Hath not God chosen the poor of this world rich in faith, and heirs of the kingdom which he hath promised to them that love him?"—James 2:5.

"Thou hast seen it; for thou beholdest mischief and spite, to requite it with thy hand: the poor committeth himself unto thee; thou art the helper of the fatherless."—Psalm 10:14.

Poverty is the only load which is heavier the more loved ones there are to assist in bearing it.

—Jean Paul Richter

PRAYER

"Again I say unto you, That if two of you shall agree on earth as touching any thing that they shall ask, it shall be done for them of my Father which is in heaven."— Matthew 18:19.

"Therefore I say unto you, What things soever ye desire, when ye pray, believe that ye receive them, and ye shall have them."—Mark 11:24.

"Ask, and it shall be given you; seek, and ye shall find; knock, and it shall be opened unto you: For every one that asketh receiveth; and he that seeketh findeth; and to him that knocketh it shall be opened."—Matthew 7:7,8.

"I waited patiently for the LORD; and he inclined unto me, and heard my cry."—Psalm 40:1.

"And whatsoever we ask, we receive of him, because we keep his commandments, and do those things that are pleasing in his sight."—I John 3:22.

Talking to our Heavenly Father is such a privilege and is also the
most powerful force that Christians have at their disposal.
We should often take advantage of coming before
our King with our praises and petitions.

"If ye then, being evil, know how to give good gifts unto your children, how much more shall your Father which is in heaven give good things to them that ask him?"— Matthew 7:11.

"If ye abide in me, and my words abide in you, ye shall ask what ye will, and it shall be done unto you."—John 15:7.

115

"Likewise the Spirit also helpeth our infirmities: for we know not what we should pray for as we ought: but the Spirit itself maketh intercession for us with groanings which cannot be uttered. And he that searcheth the hearts knoweth what is the mind of the Spirit, because he maketh intercession for the saints according to the will of God."— Romans 8:26,27.

"Praying always with all prayer and supplication in the Spirit, and watching thereunto with all perseverance and supplication for all saints."—Ephesians 6:18.

"Pray without ceasing."—I Thessalonians 5:17.

"Confess your faults one to another, and pray one for another, that ye may be healed. The effectual fervent prayer of a righteous man availeth much."—James 5:17.

"And this is the confidence that we have in him, that, if we ask any thing according to his will, he heareth us: And if we know that he hear us, whatsoever we ask, we know that we have the petitions that we desired of him."— I John 5:14,15.

When you pray, rather let your heart be without words than your words without heart.

—John Bunyan

PROMISES OF GOD

"Let us hold fast the profession of our faith without wavering; (for he is faithful that promised;)."—Hebrews 10:23.

"For all the promises of God in him are yea, and in him Amen, unto the glory of God by us."—II Corinthians 1:20.

"Blessed is the man that walketh not in the counsel of the ungodly, nor standeth in the way of sinners, nor sitteth in the seat of the scornful. But his delight is in the law of the LORD; and in his law doth he meditate day and night. And he shall be like a tree planted by the rivers of water, that bringeth forth his fruit in his season; his leaf also shall not wither; and whatsoever he doeth shall prosper."— Psalm 1:1–3.

"Call unto me, and I will answer thee, and shew thee great and mighty things, which thou knowest not."— Jeremiah 33:3.

God has made many promises to his children, and
they are the only promises that you can count
on—every time, any time, all the time.

"For God so loved the world, that he gave his only begotten Son, that whosoever believeth in him should not perish, but have everlasting life."—John 3:16.

"He staggered not at the promise of God through unbelief; but was strong in faith, giving glory to God; And being fully persuaded that, what he had promised, he was able also to perform."—Romans 4:20,21.

"That ye be not slothful, but followers of them who through faith and patience inherit the promises."—Hebrews 6:12.

"Trust in the LORD with all thine heart; and lean not unto thine own understanding. In all thy ways acknowledge him, and he shall direct thy paths."—Proverbs 3:5,6.

"Whereby are given unto us exceeding great and precious promises: that by these ye might be partakers of the divine nature, having escaped the corruption that is in the world through lust."—II Peter 1:4.

"The Lord is not slack concerning his promise, as some men count slackness; but is longsuffering to us-ward, not willing that any should perish, but that all should come to repentance."—II Peter 3:9.

"Through faith also Sara herself received strength to conceive seed, and was delivered of a child when she was past age, because she judged him faithful who had promised."— Hebrews 11:11.

"And this is the promise that he hath promised us, even eternal life."—I John 2:25.

"Who are Israelites; to whom pertaineth the adoption, and the glory, and the covenants, and the giving of the law, and the service of God, and the promises."—Romans 9:4.

We act as if God were a pauper and could do anything simply because we do not have all of the "stuff" we think we need! Shame on us!

—Shelton L. Smith

PROSPERITY

"Beloved, I wish above all things that thou mayest prosper and be in health, even as thy soul prospereth. For I rejoiced greatly, when the brethren came and testified of the truth that is in thee, even as thou walkest in the truth."—III John 2,3.

"This book of the law shall not depart out of thy mouth; but thou shalt meditate therein day and night, that thou mayest observe to do according to all that is written therein: for then thou shalt make thy way prosperous, and then thou shalt have good success."—Joshua 1:8.

"But his delight is in the law of the LORD; and in his law doth he meditate day and night. And he shall be like a tree planted by the rivers of water, that bringeth forth his fruit in his season; his leaf also shall not wither; and whatsoever he doeth shall prosper."—Psalm 1:2,3.

God's Word tells us of two kinds of prosperity: spiritual and physical. Many wonderful Christians do not experience both. Unsaved people can experience only one.

"So shall my word be that goeth forth out of my mouth: it shall not return unto me void, but it shall accomplish that which I please, and it shall prosper in the thing whereto I sent it."—Isaiah 55:11.

"Upon the first day of the week let every one of you lay by him in store, as God hath prospered him, that there be no gatherings when I come."—I Corinthians 16:2.

"Rest in the LORD, and wait patiently for him: fret not thyself because of him who prospereth in his way, because of the man who bringeth wicked devices to pass."—Psalm 37:7.

"A gift is as a precious stone in the eyes of him that hath it: whithersoever it turneth, it prospereth."—Proverbs 17:8.

"In the day of prosperity be joyful, but in the day of adversity consider: God also hath set the one over against the other, to the end that man should find nothing after him."—Ecclesiastes 7:14.

"If they obey and serve him, they shall spend their days in prosperity, and their years in pleasures."—Job 36:11.

"For the turning away of the simple shall slay them, and the prosperity of fools shall destroy them."—Proverbs 1:32.

"And the man wondering at her held his peace, to wit whether the LORD had made his journey prosperous or not."—Genesis 24:21.

"And the LORD was with Joseph, and he was a prosperous man; and he was in the house of his master the Egyptian."—Genesis 39:2.

**Prosperity is only an instrument to be used,
not a deity to be worshiped.**
                                        —Calvin Coolidge

PURITY

"Even a child is known by his doings, whether his work be pure, and whether it be right."—Proverbs 20:11.

"If thou wert pure and upright; surely now he would awake for thee, and make the habitation of thy righteousness prosperous."—Job 8:6.

"He that loveth pureness of heart, for the grace of his lips the king shall be his friend."—Proverbs 22:11.

"Finally, brethren, whatsoever things are true, whatsoever things are honest, whatsoever things are just, whatsoever things are pure, whatsoever things are lovely, whatsoever things are of good report; if there be any virtue, and if there be any praise, think on these things."—Philippians 4:8.

"Lay hands suddenly on no man, neither be partaker of other men's sins: keep thyself pure."—I Timothy 5:22.

A good conscience at the end of the day is one of your most valuable possessions. It makes sleep peaceful and serene. Living in a Biblical manner allows just that.

"The thoughts of the wicked are an abomination to the LORD: but the words of the pure are pleasant words."—Proverbs 15:26.

"Unto the pure all things are pure: but unto them that are defiled and unbelieving is nothing pure; but even their mind and conscience is defiled."—Titus 1:15.

"And every man that hath this hope in him purifieth himself, even as he is pure."—I John 3:3.

*"But the wisdom that is from above is first pure, then peaceable, gentle, and easy to be intreated, full of mercy and good fruits, without partiality, and without hypocrisy."—*James 3:17.

*"This second epistle, beloved, I now write unto you; in both which I stir up your pure minds by way of remembrance."—*II Peter 3:1.

*"Who can say, I have made my heart clean, I am pure from my sin?"—*Proverbs 20:9.

*"The way of man is froward and strange: but as for the pure, his work is right."—*Proverbs 21:8.

*"By pureness, by knowledge, by longsuffering, by kindness, by the Holy Ghost, by love unfeigned."—*II Corinthians 6:6.

**Purity lives and derives its life
solely from the Spirit of God.**

—Hare

REBELLION

"For rebellion is as the sin of witchcraft, and stubbornness is as iniquity and idolatry."—I Samuel 15:23.

"For I know thy rebellion, and thy stiff neck: behold, while I am yet alive with you this day, ye have been rebellious against the LORD; and how much more after my death?"—Deuteronomy 31:27.

"The LORD God of gods, the LORD God of gods, he knoweth, and Israel he shall know; if it be in rebellion, or if in transgression against the LORD, (save us not this day,)."—Joshua 22:22.

"For he addeth rebellion unto his sin, he clappeth his hands among us, and multiplieth his words against God."—Job 34:37.

"An evil man seeketh only rebellion: therefore a cruel messenger shall be sent against him."—Proverbs 17:11.

Even though man has been guilty of rebellion for centuries,
in our day it has become rampant. Deliberate disregard
for the rules and regulations that govern our
actions comes at a high cost.

"Therefore thus saith the LORD; Behold, I will cast thee from off the face of the earth: this year thou shalt die, because thou hast taught rebellion against the LORD."—Jeremiah 28:16.

"And might not be as their fathers, a stubborn and rebellious generation; a generation that set not their heart aright, and whose spirit was not stedfast with God."—Psalm 78:8.

NEVER QUIT!

"Therefore thus saith the LORD; Behold, I will punish Shemaiah the Nehelamite, and his seed: he shall not have a man to dwell among this people; neither shall he behold the good that I will do for my people, saith the LORD; because he hath taught rebellion against the LORD."—Jeremiah 29:32.

"If a man have a stubborn and rebellious son, which will not obey the voice of his father, or the voice of his mother, and that, when they have chastened him, will not hearken unto them: Then shall his father and his mother lay hold on him, and bring him out unto the elders of his city, and unto the gate of his place."—Deuteronomy 21:18, 19.

"Woe to the rebellious children, saith the LORD, that take counsel, but not of me; and that cover with a covering, but not of my spirit, that they may add sin to sin."—Isaiah 30:1.

"As an adamant harder than flint have I made thy forehead: fear them not, neither be dismayed at their looks, though they be a rebellious house."—Ezekiel 3:9.

"He ruleth by his power for ever; his eyes behold the nations: let not the rebellious exalt themselves. Selah."—Psalm 66:7.

"Children, obey your parents in the Lord: for this is right."—Ephesians 6:1.

No man may safely rule but he that hath learned gladly to obey.

–Thomas à Kempis

SALVATION

"So Christ was once offered to bear the sins of many; and unto them that look for him shall he appear the second time without sin unto salvation."—Hebrews 9:28.

"That if thou shalt confess with thy mouth the Lord Jesus, and shalt believe in thine heart that God hath raised him from the dead, thou shalt be saved. For with the heart man believeth unto righteousness; and with the mouth confession is made unto salvation."—Romans 10:9,10.

"For whosoever shall call upon the name of the Lord shall be saved."—Romans 10:13.

"Let all those that seek thee rejoice and be glad in thee: and let such as love thy salvation say continually, Let God be magnified."—Psalm 70:4.

"Behold, God is my salvation; I will trust, and not be afraid: for the LORD JEHOVAH is my strength and my song; he also is become my salvation."—Isaiah 12:2.

"How shall we escape, if we neglect so great salvation; which at the first began to be spoken by the Lord, and was confirmed unto us by them that heard him."—Hebrews 2:3.

Everlasting life as given by Jesus Christ to all who put their faith and trust in Him and His shed blood for the remission of their sins. Passing from spiritual death unto life in Christ.

"For I am not ashamed of the gospel of Christ: for it is the power of God unto salvation to every one that believeth; to the Jew first, and also to the Greek."—Romans 1:16.

NEVER QUIT!

"Neither is there salvation in any other: for there is none other name under heaven given among men, whereby we must be saved."—Acts 4:12.

"For the LORD taketh pleasure in his people: he will beautify the meek with salvation."—Psalm 149:4.

"I have longed for thy salvation, O LORD; and thy law is my delight."—Psalm 119:174.

"For godly sorrow worketh repentance to salvation not to be repented of: but the sorrow of the world worketh death."—II Corinthians 7:10.

"But we are bound to give thanks alway to God for you, brethren beloved of the Lord, because God hath from the beginning chosen you to salvation through sanctification of the Spirit and belief of the truth."—II Thessalonians 2:13.

"I will greatly rejoice in the LORD, my soul shall be joyful in my God; for he hath clothed me with the garments of salvation, he hath covered me with the robe of righteousness, as a bridegroom decketh himself with ornaments, and as a bride adorneth herself with her jewels."—Isaiah 61:10.

"Who are kept by the power of God through faith unto salvation ready to be revealed in the last time."—I Peter 1:5.

**Salvation may come quietly, but we
must not remain quiet about it.**

–Unknown

SECURITY IN CHRIST

"And I give unto them eternal life; and they shall never perish, neither shall any man pluck them out of my hand. My Father, which gave them me, is greater than all; and no man is able to pluck them out of my Father's hand."— John 10:28,29.

"These things have I written unto you that believe on the name of the Son of God; that ye may know that ye have eternal life, and that ye may believe on the name of the Son of God."—I John 5:13.

"Beloved, now are we the sons of God, and it doth not yet appear what we shall be: but we know that, when he shall appear, we shall be like him; for we shall see him as he is."— I John 3:2.

"Therefore if any man be in Christ, he is a new creature: old things are passed away; behold, all things are become new."—II Corinthians 5:17.

"For the which cause I also suffer these things: nevertheless I am not ashamed: for I know whom I have believed, and am persuaded that he is able to keep that which I have committed unto him against that day."—II Timothy 1:12.

Once a person becomes a child of God, he belongs to God
from that moment on. A wonderful assurance that
one belongs to the Heavenly Father forever.

"I am the good shepherd, and know my sheep, and am known of mine."—John 10:14.

"And they said, Believe on the Lord Jesus Christ, and thou shalt be saved, and thy house."—Acts 16:31.

NEVER QUIT!

"By this shall all men know that ye are my disciples, if ye have love one to another." —John 13:35.

"But as many as received him, to them gave he power to become the sons of God, even to them that believe on his name." —John 1:12.

"Whosoever is born of God doth not commit sin; for his seed remaineth in him: and he cannot sin, because he is born of God." —I John 3:9.

"He that believeth on the Son hath everlasting life: and he that believeth not the Son shall not see life; but the wrath of God abideth on him." —John 3:36.

"If we confess our sins, he is faithful and just to forgive us our sins, and to cleanse us from all unrighteousness." — I John 1:9.

"The Spirit itself beareth witness with our spirit, that we are the children of God." —Romans 8:16.

"This is he that came by water and blood, even Jesus Christ; not by water only, but by water and blood. And it is the Spirit that beareth witness, because the Spirit is truth." —I John 5:6.

"Who his own self bare our sins in his own body on the tree, that we, being dead to sins, should live unto righteousness: by whose stripes ye were healed." —I Peter 2:24.

When I was born again from above, I received
from the Risen Lord His very life....He
completed everything for my salvation
and sanctification.

—Oswald Chambers

SELF-CONTROL

"For if ye live after the flesh, ye shall die: but if ye through the Spirit do mortify the deeds of the body, ye shall live."— Romans 8:13.

*"Blessed is the man that endureth temptation: for when he is tried, he shall receive the crown of life, which the Lord hath promised to them that love him."—*James 1:12.

"But Daniel purposed in his heart that he would not defile himself with the portion of the king's meat, nor with the wine which he drank: therefore he requested of the prince of the eunuchs that he might not defile himself."— Daniel 1:8.

*"Who are kept by the power of God through faith unto salvation ready to be revealed in the last time."—*I Peter 1:5.

*"Humble yourselves therefore under the mighty hand of God, that he may exalt you in due time: Casting all your care upon him; for he careth for you."—*I Peter 5:6, 7.

This valuable characteristic is impossible apart from the influence of the Holy Spirit in a Christian's life. The Bible furnishes the guidelines for happy living.

*"Let your moderation be known unto all men. The Lord is at hand."—*Philippians 4:5.

*"And if a man also strive for masteries, yet is he not crowned, except he strive lawfully."—*II Timothy 2:5.

*"But put ye on the Lord Jesus Christ, and make not provision for the flesh, to fulfil the lusts thereof."—*Romans 13:14.

NEVER QUIT!

"Set a watch, O LORD, before my mouth; keep the door of my lips."—Psalm 141:3.

"Charity suffereth long, and is kind....Doth not behave itself unseemly, seeketh not her own, is not easily provoked, thinketh no evil."—I Corinthians 13:4,5.

"And to knowledge temperance; and to temperance patience; and to patience godliness."—II Peter 1:6.

"If any man among you seem to be religious, and bridleth not his tongue, but deceiveth his own heart, this man's religion is vain."—James 1:26.

"Know ye not that they which run in a race run all, but one receiveth the prize? So run, that ye may obtain. And every man that striveth for the mastery is temperate in all things. Now they do it to obtain a corruptible crown; but we an incorruptible."—I Corinthians 9:24,25.

**To be disappointed in the flesh is to have
put confidence there in the first place.**

–Beverly Hyles

SIN

"Blessed is he whose transgression is forgiven, whose sin is covered."—Psalm 32:1.

"Righteousness exalteth a nation: but sin is a reproach to any people."—Proverbs 14:34.

"Therefore will I divide him a portion with the great, and he shall divide the spoil with the strong; because he hath poured out his soul unto death: and he was numbered with the transgressors; and he bare the sin of many, and made intercession for the transgressors."—Isaiah 53:12.

"Moreover the law entered, that the offence might abound. But where sin abounded, grace did much more abound."—Romans 5:20.

"Fools make a mock at sin: but among the righteous there is favour."—Proverbs 14:9.

"Keep back thy servant also from presumptuous sins; let them not have dominion over me: then shall I be upright, and I shall be innocent from the great transgression."—Psalm 19:13.

Sin is the willful transgression of God's law as expressed in the Bible.

"For I will declare mine iniquity; I will be sorry for my sin."—Psalm 38:18.

"Wherefore I say unto you, All manner of sin and blasphemy shall be forgiven unto men: but the blasphemy against the Holy Ghost shall not be forgiven unto men."—Matthew 12:31.

131

"The next day John seeth Jesus coming unto him, and saith, Behold the Lamb of God, which taketh away the sin of the world."—John 1:29.

"For I acknowledge my transgressions: and my sin is ever before me."—Psalm 51:3.

"And when he is come, he will reprove the world of sin, and of righteousness, and of judgment."—John 16:8.

"Thou hast set our iniquities before thee, our secret sins in the light of thy countenance."—Psalm 90:8.

"...for whatsoever is not of faith is sin."—Romans 14:23.

"For he hath made him to be sin for us, who knew no sin; that we might be made the righteousness of God in him."—II Corinthians 5:21.

"He hath not dealt with us after our sins; nor rewarded us according to our iniquities."—Psalm 103:10.

"Who his own self bare our sins in his own body on the tree, that we, being dead to sins, should live unto righteousness: by whose stripes ye were healed."—I Peter 2:24.

Many young people die at an early age...
because they mock and laugh at sin.
—W. Jack Hudson

Sin will take you farther than you wanted to go, keep you longer than you wanted to stay and cost you more than you wanted to pay.
—Unknown

SPEECH

"A good man out of the good treasure of his heart bringeth forth that which is good; and an evil man out of the evil treasure of his heart bringeth forth that which is evil: for of the abundance of the heart his mouth speaketh."—Luke 6:45.

"Let no corrupt communication proceed out of your mouth, but that which is good to the use of edifying, that it may minister grace unto the hearers."—Ephesians 4:29.

"For he that will love life, and see good days, let him refrain his tongue from evil, and his lips that they speak no guile."—I Peter 3:10.

"But now ye also put off all these; anger, wrath, malice, blasphemy, filthy communication out of your mouth."—Colossians 3:8.

"The tongue of the just is as choice silver: the heart of the wicked is little worth."—Proverbs 10:20.

Those few words that slip off your tongue are indications
of what there is an abundance of in your heart.
Your speech allows you to be evaluated
and judged by all who hear you.

"The wicked is snared by the transgression of his lips: but the just shall come out of trouble."—Proverbs 12:13.

"The mouth of the just bringeth forth wisdom: but the froward tongue shall be cut out. The lips of the righteous know what is acceptable: but the mouth of the wicked speaketh frowardness."—Proverbs 10:31,32.

133

NEVER QUIT!

"A wholesome tongue is a tree of life: but perverseness therein is a breach in the spirit." —Proverbs 15:4.

"A soft answer turneth away wrath: but grievous words stir up anger." —Proverbs 15:1.

"If any man among you seem to be religious, and bridleth not his tongue, but deceiveth his own heart, this man's religion is vain." —James 1:26.

"Whoso keepeth his mouth and his tongue keepeth his soul from troubles." —Proverbs 21:23.

"Excellent speech becometh not a fool: much less do lying lips a prince." —Proverbs 17:7.

"He that covereth a transgression seeketh love; but he that repeateth a matter separateth very friends." —Proverbs 17:9.

"He that hath knowledge spareth his words: and a man of understanding is of an excellent spirit." —Proverbs 17:27.

"Let your speech be alway with grace, seasoned with salt, that ye may know how ye ought to answer every man." —Colossians 4:6.

"In the mouth of the foolish is a rod of pride: but the lips of the wise shall preserve them." —Proverbs 14:3.

No one will tell a tale of scandal, except to him who loves to hear it. Learn, then, to check and rebuke the detracting tongue by showing that you do not listen to it but with displeasure.

—Jerome K. Jerome

STRESS

"I can do all things through Christ which strengtheneth me."—Philippians 4:13.

"For God hath not given us the spirit of fear; but of power, and of love, and of a sound mind."—II Timothy 1:7.

"O LORD, be gracious unto us; we have waited for thee: be thou their arm every morning, our salvation also in the time of trouble."—Isaiah 33:2.

"This poor man cried, and the LORD heard him, and saved him out of all his troubles."—Psalm 34:6.

"God is our refuge and strength, a very present help in trouble. Therefore will not we fear, though the earth be removed, and though the mountains be carried into the midst of the sea; Though the waters thereof roar and be troubled, though the mountains shake with the swelling thereof. Selah."—Psalm 46:1–3.

Extreme stress is a debilitating condition, often of our own making. No matter how it comes, the Bible can help us with it. Some gain the victory over it more readily than others. However, some stress will often make us do a more thorough work.

"For the LORD your God is he that goeth with you, to fight for you against your enemies, to save you."—Deuteronomy 20:4.

"Behold, God is mine helper: the Lord is with them that uphold my soul."—Psalm 54:4.

NEVER QUIT!

"My heart is sore pained within me: and the terrors of death are fallen upon me. Fearfulness and trembling are come upon me, and horror hath overwhelmed me....As for me, I will call upon God; and the LORD shall save me."—Psalm 55:4,5,16.

"I sought the LORD, and he heard me, and delivered me from all my fears."—Psalm 34:4.

"Let not your heart be troubled: ye believe in God, believe also in me."—John 14:1.

"These things I have spoken unto you, that in me ye might have peace. In the world ye shall have tribulation: but be of good cheer; I have overcome the world."—John 16:33.

"For I reckon that the sufferings of this present time are not worthy to be compared with the glory which shall be revealed in us."—Romans 8:18.

"Rejoice evermore. Pray without ceasing. In every thing give thanks: for this is the will of God in Christ Jesus concerning you."—I Thessalonians 5:16–18.

"Trust in the LORD with all thine heart; and lean not unto thine own understanding. In all thy ways acknowledge him, and he shall direct thy paths."—Proverbs 3:5,6.

Since stress is associated with all types of activity, we could avoid it only never doing anything. Who would enjoy a life consisting of "no runs, no hits and no errors"?
–Unknown

SUCCESS

"Beloved, I wish above all things that thou mayest prosper and be in health, even as thy soul prospereth." — III John 2.

"And God is able to make all grace abound toward you; that ye, always having all sufficiency in all things, may abound to every good work." — II Corinthians 9:8.

"This book of the law shall not depart out of thy mouth; but thou shalt meditate therein day and night, that thou mayest observe to do according to all that is written therein: for then thou shalt make thy way prosperous, and then thou shalt have good success." — Joshua 1:8.

"Blessed is the man that walketh not in the counsel of the ungodly, nor standeth in the way of sinners, nor sitteth in the seat of the scornful. But his delight is in the law of the LORD; and in his law doth he meditate day and night. And he shall be like a tree planted by the rivers of water, that bringeth forth his fruit in his season; his leaf also shall not wither; and whatsoever he doeth shall prosper." — Psalm 1:1–3.

We can never really know how to measure success in the lives of everyone. It is a goal for which many of us strive but never seem to realize to a satisfactory extent.

"I can do all things through Christ which strengtheneth me." — Philippians 4:13.

"Fear thou not; for I am with thee: be not dismayed; for I am thy God: I will strengthen thee; yea, I will help thee; yea, I will uphold thee with the right hand of my righteousness." — Isaiah 41:10.

"In the house of the righteous is much treasure: but in the revenues of the wicked is trouble."—Proverbs 15:6.

"By humility and the fear of the LORD are riches, and honour, and life."—Proverbs 22:4.

"And also that every man should eat and drink, and enjoy the good of all his labour, it is the gift of God."—Ecclesiastes 3:13.

"And the LORD thy God will make thee plenteous in every work of thine hand, in the fruit of thy body, and in the fruit of thy cattle, and in the fruit of thy land, for good: for the LORD will again rejoice over thee for good, as he rejoiced over thy fathers."—Deuteronomy 30:9.

"For thou shalt eat the labour of thine hands: happy shalt thou be, and it shall be well with thee."—Psalm 128:2.

"Every man also to whom God hath given riches and wealth, and hath given him power to eat thereof, and to take his portion, and to rejoice in his labour; this is the gift of God."—Ecclesiastes 5:19.

"Commit thy works unto the LORD, and thy thoughts shall be established."—Proverbs 16:3.

Success is on the same road as failure; success is just a little farther down the road.

—Jack Hyles

TALEBEARING

"The words of a talebearer are as wounds, and they go down into the innermost parts of the belly."—Proverbs 18:8.

"Thy tongue deviseth mischiefs; like a sharp razor, working deceitfully."—Psalm 52:2.

"A talebearer revealeth secrets: but he that is of a faithful spirit concealeth the matter."—Proverbs 11:13.

"The north wind driveth away rain: so doth an angry countenance a backbiting tongue."—Proverbs 25:23.

"A froward man soweth strife: and a whisperer separateth chief friends."—Proverbs 16:28.

The most vicious activity that human beings can be
engaged in. Telling things that may or may not
be true and that do not need to be told.

"Keep thy tongue from evil, and thy lips from speaking guile."—Psalm 34:13.

"Where no wood is, there the fire goeth out: so where there is no talebearer, the strife ceaseth. As coals are to burning coals, and wood to fire; so is a contentious man to kindle strife. The words of a talebearer are as wounds, and they go down into the innermost parts of the belly."—Proverbs 26:20–22.

"For he that will love life, and see good days, let him refrain his tongue from evil, and his lips that they speak no guile."—I Peter 3:10.

"If any man among you seem to be religious, and bridleth not his tongue, but deceiveth his own heart, this man's religion is vain."—James 1:26.

"And the tongue is a fire, a world of iniquity: so is the tongue among our members, that it defileth the whole body, and setteth on fire the course of nature; and it is set on fire of hell. For every kind of beasts, and of birds, and of serpents, and of things in the sea, is tamed, and hath been tamed of mankind: But the tongue can no man tame; it is an unruly evil, full of deadly poison."—James 3:6–8.

Your "friend" who relates to you unkind information *about* another will probably relate unkind information about you *to* another.

—Lindsay Terry

TEMPTATION

"Submit yourselves therefore to God. Resist the devil, and he will flee from you."—James 4:7.

"And lead us not into temptation, but deliver us from evil: For thine is the kingdom, and the power, and the glory, for ever. Amen."—Matthew 6:13.

"Let not sin therefore reign in your mortal body, that ye should obey it in the lusts thereof. Neither yield ye your members as instruments of unrighteousness unto sin: but yield yourselves unto God, as those that are alive from the dead, and your members as instruments of righteousness unto God."—Romans 6:12,13.

"But evil men and seducers shall wax worse and worse, deceiving, and being deceived."—II Timothy 3:13.

The Word of God, rooted and grounded in your heart,
can help you with temptation more than any other
power. A test of spiritual character.

"My son, if sinners entice thee, consent thou not."—Proverbs 1:10.

"Enter not into the path of the wicked, and go not in the way of evil men. Avoid it, pass not by it, turn from it, and pass away."—Proverbs 4:14,15.

"Let no man say when he is tempted, I am tempted of God: for God cannot be tempted with evil, neither tempteth he any man. But every man is tempted, when he is drawn away of his own lust, and enticed."—James 1:13,14.

"Put on the whole armour of God, that ye may be able to stand against the wiles of the devil."—Ephesians 6:11.

"Whoso causeth the righteous to go astray in an evil way, he shall fall himself into his own pit: but the upright shall have good things in possession."—Proverbs 28:10.

"For the grace of God that bringeth salvation hath appeared to all men, Teaching us that, denying ungodliness and worldly lusts, we should live soberly, righteously, and godly, in this present world."—Titus 2:11,12.

"My brethren, count it all joy when ye fall into divers temptations; Knowing this, that the trying of your faith worketh patience."—James 1:2,3.

"There hath no temptation taken you but such as is common to man: but God is faithful, who will not suffer you to be tempted above that ye are able; but will with the temptation also make a way to escape, that ye may be able to bear it."—I Corinthians 10:13.

Apart from God we are as weak as water.
—Unknown

We are never strong enough to risk walking into temptation.
—Unknown

THANKFULNESS

"Now he that ministereth seed to the sower both minister bread for your food, and multiply your seed sown, and increase the fruits of your righteousness;) Being enriched in every thing to all bountifulness, which causeth through us thanksgiving to God. For the administration of this service not only supplieth the want of the saints, but is abundant also by many thanksgivings unto God....Thanks be unto God for his unspeakable gift."—II Corinthians 9:10–12,15.

"For all things are for your sakes, that the abundant grace might through the thanksgiving of many redound to the glory of God."—II Corinthians 4:15.

"Enter into his gates with thanksgiving, and into his courts with praise: be thankful unto him, and bless his name."—Psalm 100:4.

"That I may publish with the voice of thanksgiving, and tell of all thy wondrous works."—Psalm 26:7.

"For the LORD shall comfort Zion: he will comfort all her waste places; and he will make her wilderness like Eden, and her desert like the garden of the LORD; joy and gladness shall be found therein, thanksgiving, and the voice of melody."—Isaiah 51:3.

A Christian cannot afford to appear ungrateful if he is to keep a good testimony for Christ. One of the most wretched people on earth is the one who is without gratitude.

"Continue in prayer, and watch in the same with thanksgiving."—Colossians 4:2.

"For every creature of God is good, and nothing to be refused, if it be received with thanksgiving."—I Timothy 4:4.

"And offer a sacrifice of thanksgiving with leaven, and proclaim and publish the free offerings: for this liketh you, O ye children of Israel, saith the Lord GOD."—Amos 4:5.

"I will praise the name of God with a song, and will magnify him with thanksgiving."—Psalm 69:30.

"I will offer to thee the sacrifice of thanksgiving, and will call upon the name of the LORD."—Psalm 116:17.

"But I will sacrifice unto thee with the voice of thanksgiving; I will pay that that I have vowed. Salvation is of the LORD."—Jonah 2:9.

"But thanks be to God, which giveth us the victory through our Lord Jesus Christ."—I Corinthians 15:57.

"Giving thanks always for all things unto God and the Father in the name of our Lord Jesus Christ."—Ephesians 5:20.

"We are bound to thank God always for you, brethren, as it is meet, because that your faith groweth exceedingly, and the charity of every one of you all toward each other aboundeth."—II Thessalonians 1:3.

"I thank my God always on your behalf, for the grace of God which is given you by Jesus Christ."—I Corinthians 1:4.

Gratitude to God makes even a temporal blessing a taste of heaven.

—William Romaine

THOUGHTS

Where you really live—really!
Some are intentional, while others are not.

"Casting down imaginations, and every high thing that exalteth itself against the knowledge of God, and bringing into captivity every thought to the obedience of Christ."— II Corinthians 10:5.

"If ye then be risen with Christ, seek those things which are above, where Christ sitteth on the right hand of God. Set your affection on things above, not on things on the earth."— Colossians 3:1,2.

"For who hath known the mind of the Lord, that he may instruct him? But we have the mind of Christ."— I Corinthians 2:16.

"But so much the more went there a fame abroad of him: and great multitudes came together to hear, and to be healed by him of their infirmities. And he withdrew himself into the wilderness, and prayed."—Luke 5:15,16.

"And be not conformed to this world: but be ye transformed by the renewing of your mind, that ye may prove what is that good, and acceptable, and perfect, will of God."—Romans 12:2.

"For the word of God is quick, and powerful, and sharper than any twoedged sword, piercing even to the dividing asunder of soul and spirit, and of the joints and marrow, and is a discerner of the thoughts and intents of the heart."—Hebrews 4:12.

"A merry heart doeth good like a medicine: but a broken spirit drieth the bones."—Proverbs 17:22.

"Let the wicked forsake his way, and the unrighteous man his thoughts: and let him return unto the LORD, and he will have mercy upon him; and to our God, for he will abundantly pardon. For my thoughts are not your thoughts, neither are your ways my ways, saith the LORD. For as the heavens are higher than the earth, so are my ways higher than your ways, and my thoughts than your thoughts."—Isaiah 55:7–9.

"The thought of foolishness is sin: and the scorner is an abomination to men."—Proverbs 24:9.

"The thoughts of the righteous are right: but the counsels of the wicked are deceit."—Proverbs 12:5.

"And again, The Lord knoweth the thoughts of the wise, that they are vain."—I Corinthians 3:20.

"I know that thou canst do every thing, and that no thought can be withholden from thee."—Job 42:2.

"The LORD knoweth the thoughts of man, that they are vanity."—Psalm 94:11.

God's cure for evil thinking is to fill our minds with that which is good.

–George Sweeting

TIME

"So teach us to number our days, that we may apply our hearts unto wisdom."—Psalm 90:12.

"Walk in wisdom toward them that are without, redeeming the time."—Colossians 4:5.

"Redeeming the time, because the days are evil."—Ephesians 5:16.

"And that, knowing the time, that now it is high time to awake out of sleep: for now is our salvation nearer than when we believed."—Romans 13:11.

"And as he reasoned of righteousness, temperance, and judgment to come, Felix trembled, and answered, Go thy way for this time; when I have a convenient season, I will call for thee."—Acts 24:25.

What our lives consists of:
Queen Elizabeth's last words were reportedly,
"All my possessions for a moment of time."

"Six days shalt thou labour, and do all thy work: But the seventh day is the sabbath of the LORD thy God: in it thou shalt not do any work, thou, nor thy son, nor thy daughter, thy manservant, nor thy maidservant, nor thy cattle, nor thy stranger that is within thy gates."—Exodus 20:9,10.

"Rejoice, O young man, in thy youth; and let thy heart cheer thee in the days of thy youth, and walk in the ways of thine heart, and in the sight of thine eyes: but know thou, that for all these things God will bring thee into judgment."—Ecclesiastes 11:9.

"(For he saith, I have heard thee in a time accepted, and in the day of salvation have I succoured thee: behold, now is the accepted time; behold, now is the day of salvation.)"— II Corinthians 6:2.

"Sow to yourselves in righteousness, reap in mercy; break up your fallow ground: for it is time to seek the LORD, till he come and rain righteousness upon you."—Hosea 10:12.

"Repent ye therefore, and be converted, that your sins may be blotted out, when the times of refreshing shall come from the presence of the Lord."—Acts 3:19.

"Thus saith the LORD, In an acceptable time have I heard thee, and in a day of salvation have I helped thee: and I will preserve thee, and give thee for a covenant of the people, to establish the earth, to cause to inherit the desolate heritages."—Isaiah 49:8.

Our greatest danger in life is in permitting the urgent things to crowd out the important.

–Charles E. Hummel

Lost wealth may be replaced by industry; lost knowledge, by study; lost health, by temperance or medicine; but lost time is gone forever.

–S. Smiles

TROUBLE

"I will be glad and rejoice in thy mercy: for thou hast considered my trouble; thou hast known my soul in adversities; And hast not shut me up into the hand of the enemy: thou hast set my feet in a large room. Have mercy upon me, O LORD, for I am in trouble: mine eye is consumed with grief, yea, my soul and my belly."—Psalm 31:7–9.

"But the salvation of the righteous is of the LORD: he is their strength in the time of trouble. And the LORD shall help them, and deliver them: he shall deliver them from the wicked, and save them, because they trust in him."—Psalm 37:39, 40.

"God is our refuge and strength, a very present help in trouble."—Psalm 46:1.

"Man that is born of a woman is of few days, and full of trouble."—Job 14:1.

"The LORD also will be a refuge for the oppressed, a refuge in times of trouble."—Psalm 9:9.

"Cast thy burden upon the LORD, and he shall sustain thee: he shall never suffer the righteous to be moved."—Psalm 55:22.

The propensity for getting into trouble and the ability to get
out of it are not often characteristics of the same person.
Trouble is a great teacher! Often of my own making,
but occasionally thrust on me.

"Peace I leave with you, my peace I give unto you: not as the world giveth, give I unto you. Let not your heart be troubled, neither let it be afraid."— John 14:27.

NEVER QUIT!

"The LORD is my rock, and my fortress, and my deliverer; my God, my strength, in whom I will trust; my buckler, and the horn of my salvation, and my high tower. I will call upon the LORD, who is worthy to be praised: so shall I be saved from mine enemies."—Psalm 18:2, 3.

"Blessed be God, even the Father of our Lord Jesus Christ, the Father of mercies, and the God of all comfort; Who comforteth us in all our tribulation, that we may be able to comfort them which are in any trouble, by the comfort wherewith we ourselves are comforted of God."— II Corinthians 1:3, 4.

"Though I walk in the midst of trouble, thou wilt revive me: thou shalt stretch forth thine hand against the wrath of mine enemies, and thy right hand shall save me. The LORD will perfect that which concerneth me: thy mercy, O LORD, endureth for ever: forsake not the works of thine own hands."—Psalm 138:7, 8.

"Yea, though I walk through the valley of the shadow of death, I will fear no evil: for thou art with me; thy rod and thy staff they comfort me."—Psalm 23:4.

"Whoso keepeth his mouth and his tongue keepeth his soul from troubles."—Proverbs 21:23.

Don't look at times of testing and be bitter; don't look away from them and refuse to face reality; look through times of testing and see God.

–Jack Hyles

On dealing with the "what if" factor: "I am an old man and have known a great many troubles, but most of them never happened."

–Mark Twain

150

TRUTHFULNESS

"These are the things that ye shall do; Speak ye every man the truth to his neighbour; execute the judgment of truth and peace in your gates."—Zechariah 8:16.

"A true witness delivereth souls: but a deceitful witness speaketh lies."—Proverbs 14:25.

"He that speaketh truth sheweth forth righteousness: but a false witness deceit."—Proverbs 12:17.

"A man that beareth false witness against his neighbour is a maul, and a sword, and a sharp arrow."—Proverbs 25:18.

"I have chosen the way of truth: thy judgments have I laid before me."—Psalm 119:30.

When lying sees it, it will run away and hide.

"He is the Rock, his work is perfect: for all his ways are judgment: a God of truth and without iniquity, just and right is he."—Deuteronomy 32:4.

"The lip of truth shall be established for ever: but a lying tongue is but for a moment."—Proverbs 12:19.

"He that walketh uprightly, and worketh righteousness, and speaketh the truth in his heart."—Psalm 15:2.

"Jesus saith unto him, I am the way, the truth, and the life: no man cometh unto the Father, but by me."—John 14:6.

"But speaking the truth in love, may grow up into him in all things, which is the head, even Christ."—Ephesians 4:15.

151

"Howbeit when he, the Spirit of truth, is come, he will guide you into all truth: for he shall not speak of himself; but whatsoever he shall hear, that shall he speak: and he will shew you things to come."—John 16:13.

"And ye shall know the truth, and the truth shall make you free."—John 8:32.

"Study to shew thyself approved unto God, a workman that needeth not to be ashamed, rightly dividing the word of truth."—II Timothy 2:15.

"Rejoiceth not in iniquity, but rejoiceth in the truth."—I Corinthians 13:6.

"For of this sort are they which creep into houses, and lead captive silly women laden with sins, led away with divers lusts, Ever learning, and never able to come to the knowledge of the truth."—II Timothy 3:6, 7.

The truth is incontrovertible. Malice may attack it. Ignorance may deride it. But in the end, there it is.

—Winston Churchill

VANITY

"Woe unto them that are wise in their own eyes, and prudent in their own sight!"—Isaiah 5:21.

"For when they speak great swelling words of vanity, they allure through the lusts of the flesh, through much wantonness, those that were clean escaped from them who live in error."—II Peter 2:18.

"Where is boasting then? It is excluded. By what law? of works? Nay: but by the law of faith."—Romans 3:27.

"An high look, and a proud heart, and the plowing of the wicked, is sin."—Proverbs 21:4.

"The fear of the LORD is to hate evil: pride, and arrogancy, and the evil way, and the froward mouth, do I hate."—Proverbs 8:13.

God hates a proud look. Some take pride in the quality of their tasks, either for their family, their church or their secular jobs. We are not dealing with the latter here.

"Let nothing be done through strife or vainglory; but in lowliness of mind let each esteem other better than themselves."—Philippians 2:3.

"For all that is in the world, the lust of the flesh, and the lust of the eyes, and the pride of life, is not of the Father, but is of the world."—I John 2:16.

"But he giveth more grace. Wherefore he saith, God resisteth the proud, but giveth grace unto the humble."—James 4:6.

"Remove far from me vanity and lies: give me neither poverty nor riches; feed me with food convenient for me."—Proverbs 30:8.

"For I say, through the grace given unto me, to every man that is among you, not to think of himself more highly than he ought to think; but to think soberly, according as God hath dealt to every man the measure of faith."—Romans 12:3.

"Likewise, ye younger, submit yourselves unto the elder. Yea, all of you be subject one to another, and be clothed with humility: for God resisteth the proud, and giveth grace to the humble. Humble yourselves therefore under the mighty hand of God, that he may exalt you in due time."—I Peter 5:5,6.

"When pride cometh, then cometh shame: but with the lowly is wisdom."—Proverbs 11:2.

"Pride goeth before destruction, and an haughty spirit before a fall. Better it is to be of an humble spirit with the lowly, than to divide the spoil with the proud."—Proverbs 16:18,19.

Nothing is as hard to do gracefully as getting down off your high horse.
—Franklin P. Jones

"Remove far from me vanity and lies: give me neither poverty nor riches; feed me with food convenient for me."— Proverbs 30:8.

"For I say, through the grace given unto me, to every man that is among you, not to think of himself more highly than he ought to think; but to think soberly, according as God hath dealt to every man the measure of faith."— Romans 12:3.

"Likewise, ye younger, submit yourselves unto the elder. Yea, all of you be subject one to another, and be clothed with humility: for God resisteth the proud, and giveth grace to the humble. Humble yourselves therefore under the mighty hand of God, that he may exalt you in due time."— I Peter 5:5,6.

*"When pride cometh, then cometh shame: but with the lowly is wisdom."—*Proverbs 11:2.

"Pride goeth before destruction, and an haughty spirit before a fall. Better it is to be of an humble spirit with the lowly, than to divide the spoil with the proud."— Proverbs 16:18,19.

Nothing is as hard to do gracefully as getting down off your high horse.
—Franklin P. Jones

"Yea, if thou criest after knowledge, and liftest up thy voice for understanding; If thou seekest her as silver, and searchest for her as for hid treasures; Then shalt thou understand the fear of the LORD, and find the knowledge of God."—Proverbs 2:3–5.

"And this is the confidence that we have in him, that, if we ask any thing according to his will, he heareth us."—I John 5:1.

"For whosoever shall do the will of God, the same is my brother, and my sister, and mother."—Mark 3:35.

"In whom also we have obtained an inheritance, being predestinated according to the purpose of him who worketh all things after the counsel of his own will."—Ephesians 1:11.

"God also bearing them witness, both with signs and wonders, and with divers miracles, and gifts of the Holy Ghost, according to his own will?"—Hebrews 2:4.

God has a will for every single person, and He wants you to know His will. Life will be uncertain until you can say, "This, I know, is the will of God for my life."

—Lee Roberson

WISDOM

"The fear of the LORD is the beginning of wisdom: a good understanding have all they that do his commandments: his praise endureth for ever."—Psalm 111:10.

"Wisdom is the principal thing; therefore get wisdom: and with all thy getting get understanding."—Proverbs 4:7.

"How much better is it to get wisdom than gold! and to get understanding rather to be chosen than silver!"—Proverbs 16:16.

"The fear of the LORD is the beginning of wisdom: and the knowledge of the holy is understanding."—Proverbs 9:10.

"He that getteth wisdom loveth his own soul: he that keepeth understanding shall find good."—Proverbs 19:8.

As we move along life's way, we gain knowledge. Wisdom
is a God-given ability to use that knowledge in a
manner that will please Him.

"See then that ye walk circumspectly, not as fools, but as wise, Redeeming the time, because the days are evil."—Ephesians 5:15, 16.

"For the wisdom of this world is foolishness with God. For it is written, He taketh the wise in their own craftiness."—I Corinthians 3:19.

"For this cause we also, since the day we heard it, do not cease to pray for you, and to desire that ye might be filled with the knowledge of his will in all wisdom and spiritual understanding."—Colossians 1:9.

"But the wisdom that is from above is first pure, then peaceable, gentle, and easy to be intreated, full of mercy and good fruits, without partiality, and without hypocrisy."—James 3:17.

"Walk in wisdom toward them that are without, redeeming the time."—Colossians 4:5.

"O the depth of the riches both of the wisdom and knowledge of God! how unsearchable are his judgments, and his ways past finding out!"—Romans 11:33.

"A wise man will hear, and will increase learning; and a man of understanding shall attain unto wise counsels."—Proverbs 1:5.

"Be of the same mind one toward another. Mind not high things, but condescend to men of low estate. Be not wise in your own conceits."—Romans 12:16.

"And that from a child thou hast known the holy scriptures, which are able to make thee wise unto salvation through faith which is in Christ Jesus."—II Timothy 3:15.

Wisdom…teaches us to do as well as to talk, and to make our words and actions all of a color.

–Seneca

WITNESSING

Telling others, as groups or as individuals, the Good
News of Jesus and His love for the souls of men.

*"And Jesus said unto them, Come ye after me, and I will
make you to become fishers of men."*—Mark 1:17.

*"And daily in the temple, and in every house, they ceased
not to teach and preach Jesus Christ."*—Acts 5:42.

*"And that repentance and remission of sins should be
preached in his name among all nations, beginning at
Jerusalem."*—Luke 24:47.

*"And he commanded us to preach unto the people, and to
testify that it is he which was ordained of God to be the
Judge of quick and dead."*—Acts 10:42.

"Let the redeemed of the LORD *say so, whom he hath
redeemed from the hand of the enemy."*—Psalm 107:2.

*"And he said unto them, Go ye into all the world, and
preach the gospel to every creature."*—Mark 16:15.

*"And others save with fear, pulling them out of the fire;
hating even the garment spotted by the flesh."*—Jude 23.

*"And with great power gave the apostles witness of the
resurrection of the Lord Jesus: and great grace was upon
them all."*—Acts 4:33.

*"And they that be wise shall shine as the brightness of the
firmament; and they that turn many to righteousness as the
stars for ever and ever."*—Daniel 12:3.

NEVER QUIT!

"How then shall they call on him in whom they have not believed? and how shall they believe in him of whom they have not heard? and how shall they hear without a preacher? And how shall they preach, except they be sent? as it is written, How beautiful are the feet of them that preach the gospel of peace, and bring glad tidings of good things!"—Romans 10:14, 15.

"But sanctify the Lord God in your hearts: and be ready always to give an answer to every man that asketh you a reason of the hope that is in you with meekness and fear."—I Peter 3:15.

"For our gospel came not unto you in word only, but also in power, and in the Holy Ghost, and in much assurance; as ye know what manner of men we were among you for your sake."—I Thessalonians 1:5.

"And the lord said unto the servant, Go out into the highways and hedges, and compel them to come in, that my house may be filled."—Luke 14:23.

"Preach the word; be instant in season, out of season; reprove, rebuke, exhort with all longsuffering and doctrine."—II Timothy 4:2.

The world is far more ready to receive the Gospel than Christians are to hand it out.

–George W. Peters

WORRY

"For God hath not given us the spirit of fear; but of power, and of love, and of a sound mind." —II Timothy 1:7.

"Humble yourselves therefore under the mighty hand of God, that he may exalt you in due time: Casting all your care upon him; for he careth for you." —I Peter 5:6, 7.

"Be careful for nothing; but in every thing by prayer and supplication with thanksgiving let your requests be made known unto God. And the peace of God, which passeth all understanding, shall keep your hearts and minds through Christ Jesus." —Philippians 4:6, 7.

"And Moses said unto the people, Fear ye not, stand still, and see the salvation of the LORD, which he will shew to you to day: for the Egyptians whom ye have seen to day, ye shall see them again no more for ever." —Exodus 14:13.

"Fret not thyself because of evildoers, neither be thou envious against the workers of iniquity." —Psalm 37:1.

Worry, or anxiety, is the result of trouble with the "what if"
factor. All too often those things that we worried about
yesterday did not come to pass—and even if they
did, worrying didn't slow their pace.

"He only is my rock and my salvation: he is my defence; I shall not be moved." —Psalm 62:6.

"Therefore I say unto you, Take no thought for your life, what ye shall eat, or what ye shall drink; nor yet for your body, what ye shall put on. Is not the life more than meat, and the body than raiment?" —Matthew 6:25.

161

NEVER QUIT!

"Trust in the LORD, and do good; so shalt thou dwell in the land, and verily thou shalt be fed."—Psalm 37:3.

"For the thing which I greatly feared is come upon me, and that which I was afraid of is come unto me."—Job 3:25.

"Rest in the LORD, and wait patiently for him: fret not thyself because of him who prospereth in his way, because of the man who bringeth wicked devices to pass."—Psalm 37:7.

"I will not be afraid of ten thousands of people, that have set themselves against me round about."—Psalm 3:6.

"The LORD is on my side; I will not fear: what can man do unto me?"—Psalm 118:6.

"When thou liest down, thou shalt not be afraid: yea, thou shalt lie down, and thy sleep shall be sweet."—Proverbs 3:24.

"Behold, God is my salvation; I will trust, and not be afraid: for the LORD JEHOVAH is my strength and my song; he also is become my salvation."—Isaiah 12:2.

"Take therefore no thought for the morrow: for the morrow shall take thought for the things of itself. Sufficient unto the day is the evil thereof."—Matthew 6:34.

It is not the work, but the worry, that breaks the heart of a man.

–Charles F. Weigle

WORSHIP

"It came even to pass, as the trumpeters and singers were as one, to make one sound to be heard in praising and thanking the LORD; and when they lifted up their voice with the trumpets and cymbals and instruments of musick, and praised the LORD, saying, For he is good; for his mercy endureth for ever: that then the house was filled with a cloud, even the house of the LORD; So that the priests could not stand to minister by reason of the cloud: for the glory of the LORD had filled the house of God."—II Chronicles 5:13, 14.

"Let them praise the name of the LORD: for his name alone is excellent; his glory is above the earth and heaven."—Psalm 148:13.

"Thou, even thou, art LORD alone; thou hast made heaven, the heaven of heavens, with all their host, the earth, and all things that are therein, the seas, and all that is therein, and thou preservest them all; and the host of heaven worshippeth thee."—Nehemiah 9:6.

"Neither is worshipped with men's hands, as though he needed any thing, seeing he giveth to all life, and breath, and all things."—Acts 17:25.

God alone is worthy of our worship. The definition of the word worship is "worth-ship." There are two kinds of worship: corporate and private. Both are important, but private worship seems to bring us closer to the Saviour. It is an experience that will make your heart glad.

"By him therefore let us offer the sacrifice of praise to God continually, that is, the fruit of our lips giving thanks to his name."—Hebrews 13:15.

163

"I will bless the LORD at all times: his praise shall continually be in my mouth."—Psalm 34:1.

"Let the word of Christ dwell in you richly in all wisdom; teaching and admonishing one another in psalms and hymns and spiritual songs, singing with grace in your hearts to the Lord."—Colossians 3:16.

"I will worship toward thy holy temple, and praise thy name for thy lovingkindness and for thy truth: for thou hast magnified thy word above all thy name."—Psalm 138:2.

"Sing praises to God, sing praises: sing praises unto our King, sing praises. For God is the King of all the earth: sing ye praises with understanding."—Psalm 47:6, 7.

"Saying, I will declare thy name unto my brethren, in the midst of the church will I sing praise unto thee."—Hebrews 2:12.

"But as for me, I will come into thy house in the multitude of thy mercy: and in thy fear will I worship toward thy holy temple."—Psalm 5:7.

"O praise the LORD, all ye nations: praise him, all ye people. For his merciful kindness is great toward us: and the truth of the LORD endureth for ever. Praise ye the LORD."—Psalm 117.

Worship that is accepted by God is a privilege unique to the Christian. It is not a right. I am permitted to offer acceptable worship only by the grace of God.

–Unknown

YOUNG PEOPLE

"Remember now thy Creator in the days of thy youth, while the evil days come not, nor the years draw nigh, when thou shalt say, I have no pleasure in them."—Ecclesiastes 12:1.

"Remember not the sins of my youth, nor my transgressions: according to thy mercy remember thou me for thy goodness' sake, O LORD."—Psalm 25:7.

"Let no man despise thy youth; but be thou an example of the believers, in word, in conversation, in charity, in spirit, in faith, in purity."—I Timothy 4:12.

"Flee also youthful lusts: but follow righteousness, faith, charity, peace, with them that call on the Lord out of a pure heart."—II Timothy 2:22.

"For thou art my hope, O Lord GOD: thou art my trust from my youth."—Psalm 71:5.

There is no one quite like a bright, cheerful, energetic, Christian teenager in his or her vital, impressionable years.

"And in all thine abominations and thy whoredoms thou hast not remembered the days of thy youth, when thou wast naked and bare, and wast polluted in thy blood."—Ezekiel 16:22.

"My manner of life from my youth, which was at the first among mine own nation at Jerusalem, know all the Jews."—Acts 26:4.

"O God, thou hast taught me from my youth: and hitherto have I declared thy wondrous works."—Psalm 71:17.

NEVER QUIT!

"Foolishness is bound in the heart of a child; but the rod of correction shall drive it far from him."—Proverbs 22:15.

"Whoso keepeth the law is a wise son: but he that is a companion of riotous men shameth his father."—Proverbs 28:7.

"That they may teach the young women to be sober, to love their husbands, to love their children."—Titus 2:4.

"Who satisfieth thy mouth with good things; so that thy youth is renewed like the eagle's."—Psalm 103:5.

The error of youth is to believe that intelligence is a substitute for experience, while the error of age is to believe that experience is a substitute for intelligence.

—Wayne Mackey